EMERSON TODAY

LONDON: HUMPHREY MILFORD
OXFORD UNIVERSITY PRESS

R W aldo Emerson.

Concord, Mass ᵗˢ ''

EMERSON TODAY

THE
LOUIS CLARK VANUXEM FOUNDATION LECTURES
PRINCETON UNIVERSITY, 1931

BY

BLISS PERRY

*Professor of English Literature, emeritus
Harvard University*

EDITOR OF

"THE HEART OF EMERSON'S JOURNALS"

AND

"SELECTIONS FROM EMERSON'S PROSE WORKS"

AUTHOR OF

"THE SPIRIT OF AMERICAN LITERATURE"

"A STUDY OF POETRY"

"WALT WHITMAN"

ETC.

PRINCETON
PRINCETON UNIVERSITY PRESS

1931

PREFACE

THE greater portion of the material presented in this volume was delivered as lectures on the Vanuxem Foundation at Princeton University in March 1931. I wish to take this opportunity of expressing my appreciation of the many courtesies of the University, with which I once had the honor of being associated.

For permission to quote from Emerson's *Works* and *Journals*, I am indebted to his authorized publishers, the Houghton Mifflin Company. For the privilege of examining the hitherto unpublished manuscripts of Emerson, I owe thanks to the present representatives of his family, particularly to Edward Waldo Forbes and to Raymond Emerson.

The frontispiece portrait is reproduced from a lithograph recently made by the Forbes Lithograph Company of Boston. It was redrawn from a very small tintype of Emerson apparently taken about the middle of the eighteen-fifties. I am particularly grateful to the Forbes Lithograph Company for their kind permission to reproduce it.

BLISS PERRY

Cambridge, April 1931.

CONTENTS

CHAPTER ONE

THE KNOWN AND THE UNKNOWN EMERSON

"Be an opener of doors to those who come after you."

EMERSON

I

EMERSON was a master of parable, and there is an open parable in the very lines of his face. His features were slightly asymmetrical. Seen from one side, it was the face of a Yankee of the old school, shrewd, serious, practical; the sort of face that may still be observed in the quiet country churches of New England or at the village store. Seen from the other side, it was the face of a dreamer, a seer, a soul brooding on things to come, things as yet very far away. I once asked Daniel Chester French, the sculptor of the statue of Emerson now in the Concord Public Library, if this well known characteristic of Emerson's features did not increase the difficulty of the sculptor's task. Not at all, he replied: all that he had to do was to project the planes of each side until they met at a point beyond the face itself.

Simple as such a reconciliation of opposites appeared to the sculptor, it presents difficulties to the biographer and critic. Emerson's character, it is true, possessed a singular unity; few men in history about whom we know as much as we may know of him, had such a flawless integrity of nature. It is possible that his mind, if rightly understood in its total activity,—if all its planes could be projected and focused properly,—would be seen to possess an inner unity and simplicity no less remarkable than his character. Many Oriental students, writing in Japan or China or India, think that they discern in Emerson's mind this ultimate and absolute unity. But Western criticism as a whole has never been so confident of it. We find it hard to reconcile the two sides of the countenance: the provincial, parochial Emerson, the complete villager of Concord, the excellent neighbor, the itinerant lecturer, the life-long saunterer in meadows and by brooks, with that other haunting aspect of his dreamer's face, bent as it were upon some long journey of the spirit and whether in the body or out of the body we cannot tell. To most of us, in most hours, it seems as if Emerson the pupil and lover of Montaigne were one kind of man, and Emerson the lover of Plato and Plotinus were another. And yet we are perfectly aware that such a dichotomy is absurd, and that criticism should at least attempt that problem of unification which Mr. French solved so triumphantly as a sculptor.

The parable of the asymmetrical features, therefore, is, like the old parable of the tribute-money, a stimulus to inquiry, a suggestion of a principle. One part of Emerson is the very image and superscription of a long-vanished Concord; and we must render to Concord the things that are Concord's. But the other part of Emerson belongs to the whole world, and has as much significance to the twentieth century, and perhaps even more, than it had to the nineteenth. If seen from one angle, Emerson is a known quantity, as clearly stamped as one of Caesar's coins, there is also an almost unknown Emerson, imperfectly apprehended by his own generation, and in spite of the multitude of books about him, still very partially understood by his countrymen today.

II

A brief review of the general drift of studies of Emerson, and of the various undertakings now in progress, is essential at this point.

Emerson died in 1882, shortly before his seventy-ninth birthday, but his real mental activity had for some years been feeble. Most of his best work was done between 1836, when he published *Nature*, and 1860, the date of *The Conduct of Life*. In this rich period came his most notable addresses, the two series of *Essays*, the *Poems* of 1847, *Representative Men*, and *English Traits*. During the 1860's he published nothing except the *May Day* volume of poems, but in 1870 he printed some delightful papers, most of them written long before, under the title of *Society and Solitude*. Thereafter he was incapable of bringing his manuscripts into any order, and it was his friend James Elliot Cabot who selected some of them for the volume entitled *Letters and Social*

Aims in 1875. Cabot also put together the three posthumous volumes of lectures and essays which, with the books already mentioned, made the complete Riverside Edition of 1883, in twelve volumes. For twenty years this remained the standard edition of Emerson's writings, until it was superseded by the Centenary Edition of 1903.

During Emerson's lifetime, no real book about him, whether critical or biographical, made its appearance, with the single exception of G. W. Cooke's volume,[1] printed in 1881. With the fastidious reticence of his race and breeding, Emerson shrank from publicity of every kind, and indeed what we call the art of "salesmanship" as practised by publishers and authors was at that period almost unknown,—Walt Whitman being in this respect, as in others, one of the pioneers. Nevertheless, the newspaper and magazine notices of Emerson's lectures and essays, and reviews of his religious and philosophical opinions, were continuous and voluminous. A single collection of contemporary newspaper and review clippings about him, gathered by one of his admirers, and now deposited in the Concord Public Library, fills a dozen volumes. Many libraries have similar collections. The French criticism of Emerson, which has always been notable, began with the essay by Philarète Chasles, in the *Revue des Deux Mondes* for 1844, which was followed by the essays of Edgar Quinet and Emile Montégut.[2] German criticism likewise began in Emerson's lifetime, notably in the essays of Herman

Grimm. English criticism in this period, while interesting, is not as significant as Emerson's recognition on the Continent. The stream of translation
of Emerson's writings into European languages,
especially French, German, Italian and Spanish,
began in the 1850's, and is just now, after eighty
years, running more strongly than ever.

The second phase of studies of Emerson began
immediately after his death and continued, let us
say, until the celebration of his Centenary in 1903.
This was the period of the first biographies. Fore-
most among these, and still an indispensable book
to the student of Emerson, was Cabot's *Memoir*[3] in
two volumes, published in 1887. Mr. Cabot, in
youth a student of philosophy in Germany, had
been an intimate friend of Emerson for fifty years.
No one, except Emerson's son Edward, has ever
made such a close study of the journals and other
unprinted manuscripts. His work in tracing the
three-fold stages of Emerson's writings, namely,
first in the journals, then as lectures, and finally in
the essays as revised for publication, was invaluable. "Official" biographies are just now under a
cloud, but in 1887 the technique of Strachey and
Maurois was unknown, and the vocabulary of the
biographical psychoanalysts had not been invented.
A year later than Cabot's *Memoir* came *Emerson in
Concord*,[4] by the late Dr. Edward W. Emerson, the
poet's son. Written primarily for the "Social Circle,"
a Concord club of which both father and son were
members, this volume aimed to present Emerson as

"citizen and villager and householder, the friend and neighbor." It is vivid, truthful, and its filial piety is touched with dry New England humor. There is also both wit and humor and adroit judgment in Oliver Wendell Holmes's book about his old friend for the American Men of Letters series.[5] The Doctor had little use for the Over-Soul, but he knew Boston, and Emerson's relation with his native city, better than most men.

While the three books just mentioned are the most significant, many other volumes of reminiscence and interpretation appeared before the turn of the century. The critical essays on Emerson during the 1880's and '90's include some brilliant criticism by Arnold, Birrell, John Morley, Leslie Stephen, and R. H. Hutton in England, by Maeterlinck in Belgium, and in the United States by Lowell, Henry James, Santayana, Burroughs, Stedman, and John J. Chapman,—to name only a few out of many. Interest in Emerson was further stimulated, during this period, by the publication of his correspondence with Carlyle, John Sterling, S. G. Ward and Herman Grimm, though it was and is not yet understood how voluminous a letter-writer Emerson had actually been.

The Centenary of Emerson's birth was celebrated in 1903. There were notable exercises in Symphony Hall, Boston, President Eliot delivering the chief address and George Edward Woodberry the Ode. There was an ironic footnote for this celebration: the committee, for a wonder, had a few hundred dollars left over, and on the motion of one of its members, the President of the Unitarian Association, it was voted to spend this money in placing a marble tablet in the old Harvard Divinity School Chapel, bearing the quotation "Acquaint thyself at first hand with Deity," to commemorate Emerson's Divinity School Address of 1838, which Emerson described in a letter to Carlyle as a mere "storm in our washbowl," but which seemed so outrageous to the leading Unitarians of 1838 that Emerson was ostracized at Harvard for nearly thirty years thereafter.

The Centenary celebration at Concord can best be described from a letter by William James, who was one of many distinguished speakers: "The weather, the beauty of the village, the charming old meeting-house, the descendants of the grand old man in such profusion, the mixture of Concord and Boston heads, so many of them of our own circle, the allusions to great thought and things, and the old-time New England rusticity and rurality, the silver polls and ancient voices of the *vieille garde* who did the orating (including this 'yer child) all made a matchless combination, took one back to one's childhood, and made that rarely realized marriage of reality with ideality, that usually only occurs in fiction or poetry. I let Ralph Waldo Emerson speak for himself. . . . Reading the whole of him over again continuously has made me feel his real greatness as I never did before."[6]

Seen in the perspective of nearly thirty years, however, the most permanent memorial to Emerson established in 1903 was the publication of the Centenary Edition of his works. It had cost Edward Emerson years of toil to revise the text and prepare the invaluable notes. For the first time readers of Emerson became really aware—though Cabot had pointed it out long before—of the integral relation between the manuscript journals, the lectures as delivered orally, and the essays in their final form. Edward Emerson's task called for exact scholarship, and his only training had been that of a country doctor and a teacher of anatomy in an art school. But his filial devotion and his naturally fine taste carried him through, and as soon as the Centenary Edition was completed, he turned with the help of his nephew Waldo Emerson Forbes to the far more difficult adventure of printing, in ten volumes, his father's journals.

Only the very few students who have examined the original manuscripts can appreciate the difficulty of bringing all this material into order. Here are the intimate records of the fifty-five years from 1820 to 1875. The famous diaries of John Wesley and of John Quincy Adams cover only a slightly longer period of time. Many of the manuscript volumes are carefully dated and indexed, but there are also many entries without date, scraps of verse evidently the first draft of poems, lists of books read, hints of books to be written, golden thoughts picked up at Walden Pond on some undated summer afternoon, conversations with Hawthorne and Thoreau and Alcott, Margaret Fuller and Ellery Channing and

Jones Very, records of travel in Europe and the Far West, piercing flashes of spiritual insight followed by prosaic notes of income from lectures or the price paid for another wood-lot. It is all there, from Plotinus to Seckel pears. Dr. Emerson resolved to publish everything of value, omitting some repetitious passages, long commonplace-book quotations, a few references to Concord neighbors whose descendants might be sensitive, and a few paragraphs of intimate family history. He was reluctant, like any gentleman of his era, to print anything about his mother, and once, when I urged him to include a passage relating how his father, in a time of financial depression after the Civil War, made a most generous contribution for the new Memorial Hall at Harvard, Dr. Emerson replied, "Oh, that was one of my father's private benefactions; I could not publish that!" And indeed a complete list of such benefactions would be a very long one.

The ten volumes of the *Journals* appeared between 1909 and 1914. They made their way slowly. A condensation in two volumes, in French, was printed in Paris by Professor Régis Michaud,[7] but it was not until 1926 that a selection in a single volume was published in the United States and England.[8] The immediate reception of such a work as Emerson's *Journals* matters little, after all; its true significance is found in the new point of view which it compels critics and biographers to take. The most recent lives and studies of Emerson are all colored

by the fresh material offered by the *Journals*. A new
phase of Emerson study began indeed with the Centenary, and at least four of the outstanding books of
this period should be mentioned here.

In chronological order, the first was George E.
Woodberry's study of Emerson for the English Men
of Letters Series in 1907; a beautifully written
book if there ever was one, and all the more suggestive for its frank disclaimer of discipleship. "I
own," confesses Woodberry, "that I have little intellectual sympathy with him in any way; but I feel
in his work the presence of a great mind. He is the
only great mind that America has produced in literature." There is singular intellectual distinction,
also, in Marie Dugard's *Ralph Waldo Emerson, Sa
Vie et Son Oeuvre*, published in Paris in 1907.
Mlle. Dugard, I have been told, went to one of the
hill towns of Italy in order to write it under the
most fitting conditions; and her book has the clarity
and precision of thought, and the perfection of
style, which we have learned to expect from French
criticism.

The third book is the vivid and incisive analysis
of Emerson's life and works published by Professor
O. W. Firkins in 1915; a difficult book for some
readers because of its verbal fireworks of epigram
and paradox, but highly stimulating, and perhaps
the most original of the twentieth century books
about Emerson. The fourth is Paul Sakmann's
Emerson's Geisteswelt, Stuttgart, 1927, as yet un-

translated into English; a masterly work of scholarship and good sense.

In selecting these books for special mention, I am not unaware of the many studies of various aspects of Emerson which have lately been published. We have new biographies by Phillips Russell,[9] R. M. Gay[10] and Michaud;[11] a charming picture of Emerson among his Concord friends by Van Wyck Brooks;[12] an acute and exhaustive investigation of Emerson's relation to Swedenborg by Dr. Clarence Hotson;[13] a clear account at last of his relations to Oriental thought in Dr. Carpenter's *Emerson and Asia*;[14] and essays and learned special articles without number. While there is no bibliography later than that compiled for the Cambridge History of American Literature in 1917, one may venture the assertion that more books have been written about Emerson in the last five years than in any five years since his death. He has suffered less than most of his contemporaries from the inevitable reaction of the twentieth century against much of the New England literature of the nineteenth century. The vogue of his friends Longfellow and Whittier, Lowell and Holmes, has seemed to grow less since their centenaries were celebrated. Measured by mere vogue, and leaving intrinsic literary values out of the question, Poe and Hawthorne seem to have held their own, while Emerson, Thoreau, Melville, Whitman and Emily Dickinson have in the last twenty years gone steadily forward.

III

In Emerson's case, at least, this impression is confirmed if one glances at the studies now in progress, and particularly at those soon to be made possible by the generosity of the Emerson family in giving access to their vast collection of unprinted letters and manuscripts. All visitors to Concord have gazed at the beautiful old house, at the junction of the "Cambridge turnpike" and the "Lexington road," where Emerson lived from 1835 until his death. Many visitors, in the last half-century, have been permitted to see his study, the front room on the ground floor at the right, where everything— books and prints and photographs and even the pens upon the little table—has been kept until very lately precisely as it was in his lifetime. Here for instance was that set of the *Waverley Novels*, for a long time the only set in Concord and loaned to readers all over the village, so that one can tell from the worn bindings which volumes were most in demand. Here was the set of Goethe in fifty-five volumes, which Emerson is said to have read through in order to please his friend Carlyle. Happy hours have been spent here by privileged lovers of Emerson in taking his favorite books from the shelves, and in reading the inscriptions and pencilled annotations. But the danger of fire was always present, and the treasures were priceless. In the past year, therefore, after long debate, the entire contents of the study have been transferred to a room con-

structed on precisely the same model in the new
fire-proof building of the Concord Antiquarian Society, a few rods away. There any properly accred-
ited scholar may now have access to Emerson's
library, and that new essays and books will be
written about his works, is certain.

Furthermore, since the recent deaths of Dr. Edward W. Emerson and Mrs. William H. Forbes,
Emerson's last surviving children, their descendants
have decided to make accessible a large collection of
letters and manuscripts essential to a full understanding of Emerson's formative years and to the
comprehension of many phases of his literary activity. The journals, for instance, are being freshly
copied, in their absolute entirety. Photostatic copies
of most of the family letters, including those addressed to Emerson as well as those written by him,
are being made. Hundreds of these letters will be
included by Professor R. L. Rusk of Columbia in
his exhaustive edition of Emerson's correspondence,
now in preparation, in which all of Emerson's letters
already printed will be listed chronologically in connection with those now to be made public for the
first time. Highly interesting are the journals and
letters of the brilliant and short-lived brothers, Edward and Charles Emerson,—"the strong, star-
bright companions." These were partially utilized
in an unfinished book by the late Sylvester Baxter
entitled *The Other Emersons*, and ultimately it is
hoped that this volume, which throws much light
upon the family mood in the 1830's, will be revised

for publication. Here too are the countless and almost indecipherable pages written by the famous and eccentric Aunt Mary Moody Emerson. Ralph Waldo's abstract of her letters and diaries, made to guide him in preparing the brief memoir which appears in his published works, fills four manuscript volumes. Here are the one hundred and seventy-one manuscript sermons of the youthful Emerson, which have scarcely been looked at since Cabot examined them fifty years ago, and reported that "in general all is within the conventions of the Unitarian pulpit." Probably this is accurate enough, but one day some theologian or antiquary will wish to make sure. Of greater interest, no doubt, are the carefully written manuscripts of Emerson's lectures, particularly those early and unprinted popular discourses on science, delivered after his first visit to Europe; together with many later lectures revealing his skilful use of illustration and anecdote for specific audiences,—devices which this master of assemblies did not always retain for the essays as finally printed.

Such a rough catalogue of the treasures soon to be made available for a new generation of special students is a curious fulfillment of the wish expressed by Professor Paul Sakmann in 1927. In his final chapter he remarked: "We have as yet scarcely the beginnings of an Emerson-Philology." The word has a horrible sound, he admits; but he mentions four essential but not as yet available sources for further materials: first, a complete and chronological collection of Emerson's correspondence; second, the manuscripts of Mary Moody Emerson; third, the manuscripts of Emerson's father and brothers; and finally, a more accurate investigation of the historical change from Calvinism to Unitarianism and from Unitarianism to Transcendentalism. Three of these four *desiderata* of a German scholar are now in the way of being provided by the descendants of Emerson, and on the fourth point enough has been published already to satisfy most readers who are not specialists in New England theology.

I make no attempt to list the various books on Emerson already in preparation, but they include a bibliography and critical survey, by a well known Japanese scholar, of all the studies of Emerson produced in Japan; a book on the relations of Emersonian doctrine to the Chinese classics; a study of Emerson's contacts with France; and one dealing with Emerson in England. The mere mention of such undertakings is enough to show that a new generation of scholars, trained in historical and literary investigation, are convinced of the significance of Emerson to our modern world. There is no danger whatever of Emerson's being forgotten, but there is always the danger that in the meticulous examination of special aspects of his work and influence the main outline of his towering personality may be lost to view. A mountain may and should be studied by geologists and meteorologists, by botanists and zoologists, by mountain climbers and photographers and painters; but each of these specialists is the victim of his own temperament and training. I met not long ago on the Trift glacier above Zermatt a couple of Swiss entomologists. I was absorbed in a new view of Monte Rosa; they were equally absorbed in collecting some tiny Alpine butterflies. Happiness for happiness, theirs was probably as perfect as mine. To every man his business and desire. Yet I suspect that in our overspecialized and distracted and generally be-devilled generation there is some virtue in simply sitting down and looking at Ralph Waldo Emerson. Whatever else may be said of him, he is a "Man against the Sky."

IV

I am aware, of course, that in thick weather we may not get the view at all, and that even in clear weather each observer is limited by his physical organization, his capacity of attention, and his power of coordinating his impressions. In a later chapter we must touch upon this matter of thick weather, the clouds of disillusionment and defeatism which shut off the view of Emerson or of any other idealist. If a man believes that there are no stars in the sky, he will naturally conclude that fine talk about hitching your wagon to a star is eccentric nonsense. But leaving this question of atmospheric conditions for later discussion, we must glance at some of the personal limitations and prejudices that still prevent many readers from getting a clear view of Emerson.

It is obvious, for instance, that he was, for better or worse, a New Englander. Americans as a whole dislike the New England climate, and feel no glow of enthusiasm for New England men; finding them, for the most part, thin and cold. Again, Emerson was undeniably a Puritan, and though it was not until the first quarter of the twentieth century that the word "Puritan" became a term of common obloquy, it has always carried an unpopular connotation. Men who do not possess the key of racial instinct or the key of accurate historical knowledge are sure to misunderstand Puritanism, and many sons of the Puritans, even though they be sound historians like Hawthorne, feel an unconquerable aversion for the type. For all such men, the fact that Emerson was descended from seven generations of Puritan ministers is sufficient to place him. He must belong, in Santayana's clever and slightly malicious phrase, to "the genteel tradition."

Furthermore, Emerson was, although for a brief period, himself a minister of a Unitarian church. No more than Milton, who was successively a Churchman, a Presbyterian, an Independent, and at last something of a Quaker, could Emerson have been held by any hitching-rope of dogma very long. But it is certain that at one time he was a Unitarian in good standing, and the members of that body, whose influence in liberalizing American religious thought has been out of all proportion with its numbers, are today very proud of him. But during Emerson's lifetime, this sectarian affiliation—broken

early though it had been—was a sharp limitation
to his influence. Students of American religious history have pointed out that the orthodox distrust of
Emerson was widespread and on the whole well
founded;[15] that his teaching had little contemporary
effect upon the followers even of Dr. James Walker
of Harvard, to say nothing of the followers of Dr.
Edwards A. Park of Andover, of Horace Bushnell
of Hartford, and of the Hodges at Princeton. The
late Dr. George A. Gordon of Boston said that he
passed through Emerson's college and heard his name
mentioned in the classroom only three times. Even
at this moment we are obliged to remember that there
are hundreds of so-called colleges where a Unitarian
or an Evolutionist is not allowed to teach. It is precisely one hundred years ago (March 4, 1831) that
Emerson wrote: "The Religion that is afraid of science dishonors God and commits suicide"; and nevertheless Dayton, Tennessee, is still very distinctly on
the map of the United States.

Another variety of personal and group prejudice
was and is due to Emerson's use, for a few years, of
the then new vocabulary of Transcendentalism.[16]
Like many readers of Coleridge and Kant in the
1830's, Emerson and a group of his friends discovered that they had now a new terminology for their
experiences,—very much as the New Testament
seems to be a new book to one who reads it in a
newly acquired language. A Transcendental Club
was formed. Emerson, like Theodore Parker and the

rest, lectured on Transcendentalism, and for a few years his writings were colored by the new vocabulary. His essays on *Nature* and the "Over-Soul" can scarcely be understood without mastering it. It was like playing an old game with cards of a new color and design; amusing, even fascinating, to the players, but amazing to the on-lookers. American Transcendentalism was an inheritance from many historical sources. It fitted the mood of the hour, but unluckily it lent itself to caricature and parody, and as applied to philosophical thought, to social experiment, and even to politics, it became a term of reproach. Even church-goers who had long bowed their heads reverently at the words "the peace that passeth understanding"—a purely Transcendental phrase— became as angry as the rest. And then suddenly Transcendentalism went out of fashion and its epitaph is now written in doctoral dissertations. At least three-fourths of Emerson's published writings have little or nothing of Transcendentalism in them. But the harm had been done. Ralph Waldo Emerson had received his label. He was henceforth "The Transcendentalist." We are familiar enough with the growth of such nicknames. I have known some veteran lovers of Wordsworth who thanked God that they rejoiced in that poet long before any one told them that Wordsworth was a "Romanticist" and a "Pantheist." There are still many students of Emerson who think that when they have decided whether he is a "monist" or a "dualist," they have him all pressed and mounted and labelled for the academic herbarium.

Labels have their value for beginners in literary criticism, but how easy becomes the fatal habit of substituting a critical abstraction for an actual knowledge of a man, and then quarrelling over the abstractions!

A still sharper quarrel than that provoked by Emerson's association with American Transcendentalism has been waged over his general philosophy. Many of his readers today deny that he is a "philosopher" at all in the strict sense of that word, although admitting his right to be called a "seer." Certainly he organized no philosophical system. But he did take sides, in one of the most ancient of all controversies, that, namely, between the senses and the so-called "moral sense." He became, or it would perhaps be more accurate to say that he was born, an advocate of Intuition, as against the report of the senses, against the claims of formal argument. Epoch-making for him was the day in his Senior year at Harvard when he set down in his journal (March 14, 1821): "I am reading Price on Morals. . . . On the 56th page, Dr. Price says that right and wrong are not determined by any reasoning or deduction, but by the ultimate perception of the human mind. It is to be desired that this were capable of satisfactory proof, but, as it is in direct opposition to the sceptical philosophy, it cannot stand unsupported by strong and sufficient evidence. I will however read more and see if it is proved or no." Whether "proved or no," this theory of "ultimate perception" of right or wrong became Emerson's life-long creed. He has a thousand variations of phrase to describe it, but his favorite phrase is the "moral sentiment." He believes that this moral sentiment lies at the core of the physical universe and of the world of thought. At the close of how many of his essays, when the issue of the debate seems doubtful, does Emerson draw out this trump card of his, and lay it quietly, benignly, on the table!

The youthful Emerson was quite right in thinking that this reliance upon Intuition was "in direct opposition to the sceptical philosophy," whether it be the philosophy of Locke and Hume, or the various materialistic and mechanistic theories of the nineteenth century. In choosing his side in this perpetual controversy, he allied himself with some profound thinkers, but it is needless to say that in the army of the Intuitionalists and believers in the Divine Immanence there are whole regiments of lunatics and fakirs and amiable visionaries who believe that what they wish to be so is so. The rocking chair of Mrs. Mary Baker Eddy is just around the corner. Emerson cannot fairly be blamed, any more than Bishop Berkeley or Bergson or Croce can be blamed, for the excesses of camp-followers. But the fact remains that he has occupied an exposed position on the citadel of idealism, and has had to bear the brunt of continual attack. "In all the encounters that have yet chanced," he once wrote, "I have not been weaponed for that particular occasion, and have been historically beaten; and yet I know all the time that I have never been beaten; have never yet fought, shall certainly fight when my hour comes, and shall beat."[17] That is surely not the tone of a man who is shouting for help.

V

No list of the prejudices and partisanships that prevent a clear view of Emerson would be complete without a mention of those inconsistencies and exaggerations which are inseparable from his life-long habit of oral expression for immediate effect upon a specific audience. It is true that he wrote endless notations in his diaries, with no thought of the public, but simply as the record of the perception of each day. These records are the raw material for his lectures, later to be reshaped for his essays. Yet the mood and the rhetoric of the speaker are dominant factors from the first. His public life began as a preacher, but after his thirtieth year he turned itinerant lecturer. In that calling he earned most of his livelihood, except what he owed to a legacy from his first wife. Thanks to the Lyceum system[18] which flourished in New England after 1830, and spread to other sections of the country, Emerson could always count upon finding an audience. In towns like Concord, Salem, and Boston he appeared annually for nearly forty years. In the then frontier posts of liberal thought like Cincinnati, Louisville and St. Louis, the visits of Mr. Emerson were the bright days of the whole year. He was the favorite lecturer of "Billy" Herndon in Springfield, Illinois, and of

Mark Hanna in Cleveland. He was a travelling merchant of certain facts and truths, displaying his wares with consummate skill, but limited on each occasion to the inexorable sixty minutes. He writes in 1837 to his old schoolmate Dr. W. H. Furness:[19] "I am wading—sometimes overhead—in the most ambitious Course of Lectures—a little precipitately undertaken—once a week on a new subject, and each subject the Universe seen from one side; so that the Lecturer's task seems to me nothing less than Puck's 'I will put a girdle round about the world in forty minutes'—say sixty rather." Some of his auditors, certainly, found him vague and incomprehensible, but no one seems to have left the hall. In the literal sense of a much-abused word, Emerson was a "spellbinder." Exactly how he wove his spell was a matter on which there is various testimony,[20] but all listeners agreed as to the radiant presence, the serene voice, the quiet manner in which he uttered startling radicalisms, steadying conservatisms, an amazing wealth of illustration and anecdote,—touched now and then with dry Yankee humor,—and epigrams and paradoxes without end. He never compromised his convictions, but he did play with his audiences as Socrates played with his pupils, taking up idea after idea, examining it as if he had never seen it before, turning it over to look at the under side of it, behaving now like a lawyer for the prosecution and then swiftly becoming a lawyer for the defense, but ending usually as a wise and gentle "counsellor for the situation"—in Mr. Justice Brandeis's phrase—

rather than as an advocate for either side. Frequently
he postpones his decision so long that you are tempted
to wonder whether he had really made up his mind.
It is only at the end of the lecture on Napoleon that
you discover that "you were not dealing with a
gentleman, at last; but with an impostor and a
rogue." It is at the very close of the lecture on Montaigne, perhaps the most brilliant defense of scep-
ticism ever written, that he drops his trump card
upon the table, with the tranquil words: "The final
solution in which skepticism is lost, is in the moral
sentiment, which never forfeits its supremacy. All
moods may be safely tried, and their weight allowed
to all objections: the moral sentiment as easily out-
weighs them all, as any one. This is the drop which
balances the sea."

Yet if one were listening so such lectures, instead
of coolly analyzing them in print, would it not seem
as if a conjurer were tossing flashing coins, care-
less of whether they fell heads or tails? The conjurer knows precisely how his coin will fall, for he
has cunningly weighted it beforehand, but how is
the audience to know? Might it not easily seem as if
the mere flashing of the golden phrases, one after
another, were the real game? Few writers of prose
have ever polished such glittering single sentences,
but the very brilliancy of the units may distract the
attention from the main drift and purpose of the
discourse. A friend of Emerson and a careful listener
to many of his lectures, once said to me that this
fascination of isolated sentences made it difficult to

grasp the lecture as a whole. Critics have made too much, I think, of the inconsecutiveness of Emerson's addresses. If one will take the trouble to brief a dozen of them, he will find that the divisions and sub-divisions are usually made with care, for that was one of the traditions of the pulpit oratory in which Emerson had been trained. Yet his friend was probably right in feeling that the discourses as delivered seemed less closely articulated than they really were.

And there is another inherent defect of the oral method which Emerson could not avoid and in which he even took delight. It is found in the obvious fact that no philosopher or sage or hot gospeller can possibly present the whole truth in any one discourse. This has been tried too often by preachers facing university congregations! The skilful practitioner, like John Wesley or Whitefield or Phillips Brooks, has learned that he must content himself with that single aspect of truth which he finds most appropriate or necessary for a specific occasion. Emerson accepted this limitation with joy. It suited his temperament, which was as "undulant and diverse" as that of his master, Montaigne. But it confirmed him in the vice of over-statement of his case. There would be other occasions, he reflected cheerfully, when he could redress the balance if necessary; and yet after all, why have any balance? We can do well enough without it. "My page about 'Consistency,' " he said in his *Journals*, "would be better written thus: Damn Consistency!"

One may enjoy such boyish recklessness, without forgetting that it frequently made trouble for his hearers and that it still troubles his readers. Suppose, for instance, that one is listening to the famous lecture on "Fate." No nineteenth century advocate of a mechanistic universe has stated with greater impressiveness the argument for materialism and determinism. The speaker marshals all the forces that make against the liberty and significance of the individual. He warns us, indeed, at the outset, that "If we must accept Fate, we are not less compelled to affirm liberty, the significance of the individual, the grandeur of duty, the power of character. This is true and that other is true." In other words, he is going to toss the coin. He keeps it in the air a long time, and one cannot tell whether it will fall heads or tails. "Nature and Thought; two boys pushing each other on the curbstone of the pavement." Which boy will win? The next lecture in the course, entitled "Power," makes it perfectly clear which boy must win at the last, and Emerson knew it at the very moment when he was stating the case for "Fate." But suppose one hears or reads only one lecture of the course? How many of the young persons who have been thrilled by the pages of "Self-Reliance" have been able to perceive, simply by the evidence offered in that essay, that Emerson always had the higher self in mind, and that, in his son's words,—he really meant "God-Reliance" when he said "Self-Reliance"?

A still better illustration of the immediacy and partiality of the oral method is found in the Divinity School Address. Emerson is trying to shock a half-dozen book-nurtured, tradition-nurtured young theologians into a sense of the reality of the living God. Like a prophet addressing professional-minded priests he cries: "God is, not was; He speaketh, not spake." This alteration of tenses seemed blasphemous to the ears of Professor Andrews Norton and Professor Henry Ware, Jr., but it is certain that some of that tiny graduating class caught the point: namely, that whoever attempts to preach about God must know Him through personal experience and not merely through books and tradition. Stated in such terms, the idea is a commonplace of the prophets of all religions. Emerson made it seem new by emphasizing personal experience only,—"acquaint thyself at first hand with Deity"—believing that for that occasion and audience a half-truth was best. A Roman Catholic priest, himself a poet and a lover of Emerson's writings, in discussing with me the Divinity School Address remarked: "If God *is*, He *was*, wasn't He? If He *speaks*, He *spake*, didn't He"? That is to say, if you postulate an eternally existent God, you must take the logical consequences. Emerson, we may be sure, would have given his smiling assent to the priest's dialectics, but on the very next occasion, he would have gambled again with a half-truth. It had worked.

But enough has been said for the moment of these various obstacles to a fair view of Ralph Waldo

Emerson. His contemporaries, like ourselves, were obliged before judging him dispassionately to make allowance for their own personal and group prejudices, their habitual modes of thinking, their dislike, or perhaps their admiration, for the peculiar forms of expression which he used. No writer or thinker, however eminent, commands the real attention of more than a very small minority of his contemporaries. Emerson's own estimate of the size and nature of his audience was characteristically modest. Writing in 1844 to Carlyle, who had prepared a striking preface to the English edition of the *Essays*, Emerson protested: "You shall not do this again, if I should send you any more books. A Preface from you is a sort of banner or oriflamme, a little too splendid for my occasion, and misleads. I fancy my readers to be a very quiet, plain, even obscure class,—men and women of some religious culture and aspirations, young, or else mystical, and by no means including the great literary and fashionable army, which no man can count, who now read your books. If you introduce me, your readers and the literary papers try to read me, and with false expectations. I had rather have fewer readers and only such as belong to me."

That the readers who belong to him have grown so steadily in numbers, in his own country and abroad, is evidence enough that the difficulties of approach to him are not insurmountable. But it is still useful to distinguish between the two Emersons, namely, the citizen of Concord, and the citizen of that other country which lies far off on the world's rim. Let

us look first, then, at the once sharply outlined figure
of a gentleman of the old school, who died nearly
fifty years ago, and is remembered today by a few
elderly persons only. But he is profitable company;
even for those who have little curiosity about Emerson the mystic and the poet.

CHAPTER TWO

THE DAILY BREAD

"Life consists of what a man is thinking of all day."

Emerson's *Journals*.

I

EVERY mountain climber knows that in certain lights, or in certain moods of the observer, the noblest peaks seem to flatten down and become mere piles of rock. Such hours, when the veils of illusion are withdrawn, are useful to the mountaineer as a corrective. Students of biography are aware of similar alternations from the mood of idealization to the plain daylight of fact. We know, for instance, that Lincoln was a mystic and a seer; but we also know that he was a corporation lawyer and an adroit politician. It is the combination of these traits that gives Lincoln his unique quality.

In the case of Emerson a similar distinction and combination must be made. The verdict of his contemporaries, his own writings, and the books written about him in many languages in each decade since his death, make it certain that he possessed a unique personal quality—an "Emersonianism," so to speak—which tends to isolate him, in our minds at least, from the other men of his period. It is the business of literary criticism to analyze this peculiarity. As Walter Pater said of Wordsworth, "What special sense does he exercise, and what instincts does he satisfy?" But it is also the task of biography, as distinguished from purely literary criticism, to point out that Emerson's roots lay deep in the common soil, that he represented a significant generation of American endeavor, and that he was a factor in the social and political as well as the intellectual history of his era. On this side also, there is a parallel in Wordsworth. The English poet wrote to one of his American friends that he had devoted twelve hours to public questions to every hour that he had devoted to poetry. Wordsworth's place in literature is due no doubt to his relatively rare moments of pure poetic ecstasy; and nevertheless, students of Wordsworth still search his *Prose Works* and his correspondence for priceless evidence of the growth of his mind and his attitude toward the England and Europe of his day. The ecstatic moment cannot be isolated from the everyday experience which underlies it.

II

For the first thirty years of Ralph Waldo Emerson's life,—let us say, until his return from Europe in 1833—his case was typical rather than markedly exceptional. It was the often repeated story of a youth of pure English stock, of long Colonial and Revolutionary traditions, growing to manhood under the stern frugal conditions of eastern Massachusetts. His earliest American ancestor on the paternal side, Thomas Emerson, was a farmer and baker who settled in Ipswich in 1635. He saved money. His son, and his son's sons for six generations, went to Harvard College and became ministers. William Emerson, Ralph Waldo's grandfather, married Phoebe Bliss, built the Old Manse at Concord about 1769, and died as an army chaplain in the Revolution. His son William, Ralph Waldo's father, was the eloquent, public-spirited, theologically liberal minister of the famous First Church in Boston. He married Ruth Haskins, daughter of a cooper and distiller who had protested against the Unitarian alterations in the King's Chapel prayerbook. When this second William Emerson died, aged forty-two, in 1811, he left a widow with six small children, five of them boys. They were poor, shy and proud. One of the boys, Bulkeley, had a childish illness which kept him mentally undeveloped. The other four, William, Ralph, Edward and Charles, went through the Boston Latin School and Harvard College. It was a family habit. Ralph, "the spiritual looking boy in blue nankeen," as his schoolmate W. H. Furness described him, made an undistinguished academic record. He was less plodding than his sober elder brother William, and far less brilliant than Edward and Charles. At twelve he could write smooth Augustan couplets, but so could many boys of that period. He could speak a "piece" well, like his father and grandfather.

He entered Harvard in 1817, under the presidency of Dr. Kirkland. He improved his Latin and Greek, and neglected his mathematics. Little or no science was then taught. Hebrew was still a required study, but French might be substituted if the student were over twenty-one (most of them were under eighteen!) or if his parents desired it. Emerson apparently took French. He heard the eloquent public lectures of George Ticknor and Edward Everett. He did a great deal of private reading, as his college journals show. The records of the Harvard Library, then kept by Professor Andrews Norton, show that "Emerson 4th"—so denominated since there were three older Emersons in college—drew in his Freshman year fourteen books, most of them sound eighteenth century history and philosophy. For the details of his college life, the *Journals* are almost the only source, but there is an interesting sketch of him in the privately printed *Reminiscences* of S. K. Lothrop.[1] Lothrop, who was President Kirkland's nephew, came to Cambridge in 1817, and lived with his uncle in Wadsworth House, while finishing his preparation for Harvard. He was tutored by young Emerson, who was then residing in Wadsworth House as "the President's Freshman,"—that is to say, an errand boy to carry official notices. "He was about two years older than myself" wrote Dr. Lothrop, who was himself only thirteen in 1817, "and nearly as tall as when he had reached maturity,—a Saxon blonde, pale face, light hair, blue eyes. He was calm and quiet in his manners, and no matter how much he felt, externally he was never moved or excited. . . . He was a very peculiar person,—kind, easy, familiar with me, but still with a wall of reserve about him which he would not let anybody penetrate; not caring much about sympathy, though

receiving it not ungraciously, and while having nothing of self-assertion, being to a remarkable degree
self-sustained, sufficient unto himself, and happy in
his own thoughts, in his own soul. He would read
me his poetry or prose, and though pleased with
the delight I expressed, there was always something
in his manner which seemed to say: 'I don't much
care whether you like them or not; they are mine;
I wrote them, and can have satisfaction in them myself.' "

In that description of Emerson at fifteen, written
by a man who never claimed to be one of his admirers, there is more than a hint of something exceptional, "a peculiar person," not to be classified
with the other undergraduates of the period. Yet it
seems doubtful whether many of his classmates recognized it. At graduation he ranked thirtieth in a
class of fifty-nine, and his biographers take a natural
ironic pleasure in reminding us that he was chosen
class poet only after six others had declined that
honor. Henri Bergson, by the way, had precisely the
same experience! It is evident that we are not dealing with a youthful prodigy, but with a slowly-
maturing, cautious, self-scrutinizing Yankee. For
seven or eight years after Emerson's graduation
one must read between the lines of the scanty record
to find the road which he is really travelling. At
first, like so many college boys of that period, he
taught school in order to pay for his own education
and that of his younger brothers. There was no flaw
in his tribal loyalty. At eighteen he was teaching

girls in his older brother William's school in Boston. At twenty-one, Ralph decided to enter the ministry. It was the ancestral profession of the Emersons, and his brother William was already studying Divinity in Germany.

The long passage in Ralph's journal (April 18, 1824) in which he records the self-examination that led to his decision reminds one strangely of the talk about learned professions in Marlowe's *Dr. Faustus*, and of the study scene in Goethe's *Faust*. He dismisses law and medicine as unsuited for him. "But in Divinity I hope to thrive. I inherit from my sire a formality of manner and of speech, but I derive from him, or his patriotic parent, a passionate love for the strains of eloquence. I burn after the 'aliquid immensum infinitumque' which Cicero desired." A little later in this long soliloquy comes the sentence in which one seems today to hear an ominous sound of thunder on the left: "I judge that if I devote my nights and days *in form*, to the service of God and the War against Sin, I shall soon be prepared to do the same *in substance*." We shall see about that.

Having earned plenty of money, at last, for his immediate needs, the youth enrolled in the Harvard Divinity School in 1825. The School was then in very low estate. It gave no degrees, in fact, until 1870. The students apparently attended lectures if and when they pleased. Emerson attended very few, for he had no sooner taken up residence in Divinity Hall than his eyes failed, and his general health gave cause for alarm. Consumption had been the family malady. He left Divinity Hall, worked on his uncle's farm, and did a little private tutoring and school-teaching; then drifted back to Cambridge. Though he had received no real professional discipline either in theology or exegesis, the Middlesex County Association of Ministers "approbated" him to preach in October 1826. "If they had examined me, they never would have passed me," Emerson said afterward. But that is by no means certain: they had known his father and grandfather, and looking into Ralph's honest blue Emerson eyes, those kindly gentlemen were ready enough to take a reasonable chance.

Within a month, however, his illness recurred, and he sailed for South Carolina and Florida for the winter. Here he made a close friend of a wholly new type, Achille Murat,[2] son of Bonaparte's King of Naples,—a charming young exile with a gift for expounding Atheism. A few family letters—some of them as yet unpublished—and a few entries in the *Journals*, record Emerson's slowly regained bodily vigor, his return to New England, his betrothal and marriage to a delicate, consumptive girl, Ellen Tucker of Concord, New Hampshire, and his call to be associate pastor of the old Second Church of Boston. He was singularly happy in his marriage, in spite of recurrent anxiety over his young wife's health. He was happy, too, in his church, and soon became its sole pastor. Like his father, he threw himself into the work for the community, serving on the School Board, as chaplain of the State Senate, and working faithfully at the Seamen's Bethel with his eccentric and delightful Methodist friend, "Father" Taylor. The sky seemed almost cloudless,—too cloudless, in fact, for a New Englander who believed that the perfect days are weather-breeders. "Can this hold," he asked his Aunt Mary on January 6, 1829;[3] and he sketches the family fortunes at this entrance upon a new year. William had been beset by doubts, while at Göttingen, over his fitness for the ministry, and though the great Goethe, whom he consulted, advised him to waive his scruples and stick to his calling, he had come home to study law. Edward had had an attack of insanity. Nevertheless Ralph Waldo writes: "Look at the altered aspect. William has begun to live by the law. Edward has recovered his reason and his health, Bulkeley was never more comfortable in his life. Charles is prospering in all ways. Waldo is comparatively well and comparatively successful— far more so than his friends, out of his family, anticipated. Now I add to all this felicity a particular felicity [his engagement] which makes my own glass very much larger and fuller. And I straightway say, Can this hold?"

We know well enough now that it did not hold. By 1831 the young wife was dead. The critics who still repeat the shallow verdict that Emerson never suffered, and could consequently preach an easy optimism, are probably ignorant of the paroxysms of grief that he endured. He threw himself manfully into his professional work, however, only to discover at last that he was out of place in any ecclesiastical organiza-

tion. The *Journals* make this very clear: (June 20,
1831) "In the Bible you are not directed to be a Unitarian, or a Calvinist or an Episcopalian. . . . If a man
is wise he will say to himself, I am not a member
of that or of any party. I am God's child, a disciple of
Christ, or, in the eye of God, a fellow disciple with
Christ. . . . A sect or party is an elegant incognito
devised to save a man from the vexation of thinking."

The specific occasion for his inevitable break with
ecclesiasticism came in 1832, when he made known to
his congregation his unwillingness to continue to
administer the Lord's Supper. He had been reading
deeply in Quaker doctrine, and his study of church
history had convinced him that Jesus "did not intend
to establish an institution for perpetual observance
when he ate the Passover with his disciples." Emerson's sermon setting forth his views,—the only sermon of his that has thus far been printed[4]—may be
commended to all readers who still think him incapable of clear statement. It is flawlessly clear,—and
in the opinion of the vast majority of Christians,
clearly wrong. We are not here concerned with the
validity of his argument, but rather with the personal
qualities which this crisis revealed. It was probable
from the first, though not certain, that the Second
Church would fail to agree with its pastor. Like
many a young prophet, he went into the wilderness
to meditate, pending the decision of the congregation, and in Ethan Allen Crawford's farmhouse in the
Crawford Notch he tried to think the whole matter
through. "The good of going into the mountains is

that life is reconsidered," he writes in his *Journals*
(July 6, 1832). "Religion in the mind is not cre-
dulity, and in the practice is not form. It is a life.
. . . It is not something else *to be got*, to be *added*,
but is a new life of those faculties you have. It is to
do right. It is to love, it is to serve, it is to think, it
is to be humble." Francis of Assisi might have said
that, or Tolstoi. And equally simple, equally final,
was the sentence of his farewell sermon (September
9, 1832), after it became clear that the Second
Church was unwilling to retain him as pastor upon
the conditions which he had laid down: "It is my
desire in the office of a Christian minister, to do
nothing which I cannot do with my whole heart."
Here is where the psychographer, trying to plow into
Emerson's character, strikes the underlying ledge
of New England granite. There was nothing more to
be said. Emerson and the members of his church
parted, with mutual respect and affection. He sent
them a farewell letter,[5]—printed, oddly enough, on
white silk,—full of tenderness and beauty. Then,
midway in his thirtieth year, he sailed for Europe.

III

If Emerson had died in that thirtieth year, instead
of sailing away to begin life over again, one wonders
what would be thought of him today,—provided
he were remembered at all. He had published almost
nothing. He had written a few verses, a private
diary, and some acceptable sermons. If his name sur-
vived for us, it might be in some volume of annals

of the New England pulpit, where, like his father
and grandfather or his contemporary the once famous J. S. Buckminster, he would be set down among
the short-lived heirs of unfulfilled renown. Fra-
grant, no doubt, would be the record, as if printed
upon faded silk: the picture of such a young clergy-
man as Hawthorne loved to draw; something graceful, ethereal, bodiless; a type rather than an
individual.

But we may dismiss such idle fancies. Emerson's
fate was not to die, but to live and to "set forth the
works of the Lord" after a new and amazing fashion. In the five years from 1833 to 1838 he found
his true vocation and challenged the prevalent
thought of New England; in ten more years—let us
say, by his return from the second visit to Europe
in 1848—he had won a national reputation, which
grew steadily and securely until the end of his life.

One who attempts, in this second quarter of the
twentieth century, to trace the grounds for a literary
reputation gained in the second quarter of the
nineteenth century, has some obvious advantage of
perspective. He looks, very naturally, for the first
expression of those distinctive ideas, the first evidence of that peculiar power over words, which
made the name of Ralph Waldo Emerson memorable. The critic of today examines Emerson's
first book, the anonymously printed *Nature* of 1836,
and points out that the essence of the Emersonian
gospel, the highly individual flavor of Emerson's
prose style, are here once for all revealed. The critic

is quite right. But he is tempted to forget that it took thirteen years to sell the first five hundred copies of *Nature;* and that meantime Emerson was making his way by virtue of other qualities than those of a mystic and poet. One does not need to say that the imaginative side of Emerson is essential to an understanding of his personality and ultimate influence, but before turning to that aspect of Emerson's mind, let us first try to see him from another angle.

The *Journals* of his European travels reveal a vigorous young man bent upon self-cultivation, upon intellectual and artistic discipline. No schoolteacher in his first visit to Europe ever worked harder, for nine months, over art galleries and cathedrals and national characteristics. He slaved away at Italian and French. He read Goethe. At the opera and theater, at dinners and at least one fancy-dress ball, on the boulevards of Paris and on the Scotch moors, he walked and talked with new types of men. His curiosity was endless. He kept to the end of his life the worn program of lectures that he attended at the Sorbonne. I found it among his papers the other day. He sought out Landor and Coleridge, Wordsworth and Carlyle, in the hope of discovering new secrets in the understanding of life. But if we were to select one epoch-making hour of his journey it might well be on that July day when he visited the museum of the *Jardin des Plantes* in Paris.

Readers of Balzac will recall that it was in the very summer of 1833 that that strange young man rushed into his sister's room and cried "Congratulate me, my dear, I am about to become famous!" For he had just discovered the scheme for his *Human Comedy*. Some students of Balzac believe,—although exact proof is difficult to establish—that his idea originated in a visit to the cabinets of natural history in the *Jardin des Plantes*. At any rate, in his Introduction to the *Human Comedy*, he wrote: "The idea [of the Human Comedy] originated in a comparison between Humanity and Animality. . . . The Creator works on a single model for every organized being. 'The Animal' is elementary, and takes its external form, or, to be accurate, the differences in its form, from the environment in which it is obliged to develop. Zoological species are the result of these differences. . . . Does not society modify Man, according to the conditions in which he lives and acts, into men as manifold as the species in Zoology? The differences between a soldier, an artisan, a man of business, a lawyer, an idler, a student, a statesman, a merchant, a sailor, a poet, a beggar, a priest, are as great, though not so easy to define, as those between the wolf, the lion, the ass, the crow, the shark, the sheep, etc. Thus *social species* have always existed and will always exist, just as there are zoological species."

Is it too fanciful to imagine the bull-necked young provincial from Tours, and the tall, blue-eyed Yankee, leaning side by side over the same cabinet, with the same new vision of the "unity in variety" of Nature dawning upon the imagination of each? Note the terms in which Emerson records the experience. His *Journals* for July 13, 1833, give the first draft, but I quote from the expanded version which he contributed to the *Gift*, an American annual of the year 1844: "The universe is a wilder puzzle than ever, as you look along this stark series of once animated forms—the hazy butterflies, the carved shells, the bird, beast, worm, snake, and fish, and the upheaving principle of life everywhere incipient, in the very rock aping organized forms. Whilst I stood there, I yielded to a singular conviction, that in all these rich groups of natural productions which surrounded me, and in all the vast system which they represented, not a form so grotesque, so savage, so beautiful, but is an expression of some property in man the observer. I felt that there is an occult relation between the crawling scorpion, the flowering zoophyte, and man. I was moved by strange sympathies. I said, "I will listen to this invitation; I also am a naturalist."

Could there be a more curious coincidence than that dawning of the same idea in the consciousness of these two men: one of them destined to work it out in naturalistic fiction, and the other destined to become a "naturalist of souls"? "To write the natural history of reason" was a task which Emerson proposed to himself in 1837,[6] and though he was unable to perform it, his Harvard lectures in 1870 were printed under the old gallant title *The Natural History of Intellect*.

And is there not a singular touch of Balzac in the sentence written by Emerson in his *Journals* (September 6, 1833) as he was sailing homewards? "I like my book about Nature." Not a line of the book had yet been written, apparently, yet the author liked it! And two days later, in a long Sunday meditation on the "wonderful congruities of the moral law of human nature" he sketched what was to prove, three years later, to be the central thought of his first book.

It was no accident, therefore, but the result of a startling experience, that Emerson chose, for his very first public discourse as a layman, on November 4, 1833, before the Boston Society of Natural History, the subject "The Uses of Natural History." It was never printed, though an examination of the manuscript shows that Cabot's outline of it is accurate. Emerson described his visit, a few months earlier, to the museum of the *Jardin des Plantes*, and the feeling it gave of the occult relation between animals and man. "It is in my judgment," said the lecturer, "the greatest office of natural science (and one which as yet is only beginning to be discharged) to explain man to himself"; and I find in the next to the last sentence of his manuscript these significant words: "The laws of moral nature answer to those of matter as face to face in a glass." He used that sentence three years later in his first book.

In the unpublished autobiography of Dr. Moses Ashley Curtis,[7] a distinguished botanist who heard, at the age of twenty-five, this first lecture, there is an interesting account of it: "Nov. 5. Attended the first of the fourth course of lectures before the Boston Society of Natural History. Price of admission to the course with the privilege of visiting the Society's Cabinet is one dollar. The lecture this evening by Rev. Ralph W. Emerson was on the advantages of the study of Nat. History. Several hundred were present and seemed highly gratified with the address. There was indeed much elegance in it, but on retrospect there seems to be very little of it that is tangible. His last topic of consideration seemed to be a kind of occult sympathy between the spirit of man and the material world, in which there was so much of a metaphysical dreaminess that I was unable to catch his meaning, neither do I suppose that himself knew what web he was weaving."

This is the earliest record I have found of Emerson as a lecturer, and its final clause anticipates one kind of criticism which is traceable throughout his public career and which continues to this day: namely, "I could not catch his meaning; ergo, there was no meaning." Nevertheless, Emerson gave three other lectures that winter before the Society: on the "Relation of Man to the Globe," on "Water" and on "The Naturalist." All these lectures remain in manuscript, and I doubt whether more than one or two persons have looked at them since Cabot examined them nearly fifty years ago. As contributions to science they are, of course, negligible, but they are highly significant as evidence of Emerson's new curiosity about our actual world. They help to explain the remark of Agassiz,[8] years afterward, that he preferred Emerson's conversation on scientific subjects to that of any man he knew.

IV

Within a year after his return from Europe we find the young lecturer settled in Concord,—at first in the Old Manse built by his grandfather, where he and his mother were the guests of Dr. Ripley, and after 1835 in a home of his own. We need not rehearse many details of the new life that opened before him. At last he was in the right place. He had his bearings. What chiefly concerns us, in this glance at his every-day experience, is its naturalness, its wholesomeness. He was writing mysticism from time to time in his private diary and on the manuscript pages of his first book, and some of his neighbors may have suspected it. Nevertheless they welcomed him as a true son of Concord into the ordinary life of the village. They put him on the School Committee. He taught in the Sunday School. He joined the Fire Company, and the Social Circle. In 1835 he was invited to deliver the historical address on the two hundredth anniversary of the settlement of the town; and a model discourse it was, based on thorough research of manuscript and printed records, and so clear that the surviving veterans of the fight at Concord Bridge, sixty years before, could follow every word of it. For forty years thereafter, Emerson's neighbors kept drafting him for similar services on occasions of local and national significance. Sometimes they drew up a formal petition, with signatures, as when they asked him to speak on the Fugitive Slave Law in 1851. They could always trust him for the right word. "Thou art a scholar; speak to it, Horatio."

On Sundays Mr. Emerson could be seen in his pew in the Unitarian church, unless, as happened often in the first decade after his settlement in Concord, he was himself filling a pulpit elsewhere. He did not administer the Lord's Supper any more, nor did he offer what was then called "the long prayer" unless he felt like it, but there is abundant testimony to the simplicity and spiritual elevation of these occasional sermons. For a long time he preached every Sunday in the tiny church at East Lexington, and it was here that one of his congregation made the delightful comment: "We are very simple people here, and don't understand anybody but Mr. Emerson." For one period of his middle life he absented himself from church. He did not enjoy his minister's discourses, and though he liked to have Mrs. Emerson and the children attend regularly, he confesses, in an unpublished letter, that he once scribbled a poem during the sermon. By slipping out of his side door and across the meadows, he could soon reach Walden Pond; and had not Henry Thoreau and Ellery Channing formed the "Walden Pond Association" as a substitute for sermons? In his old age, however, Emerson renewed the church-going habits of his youth, and as an Overseer of Harvard College he voted to retain required attendance at Chapel, although Phillips Brooks and a majority of the Overseers voted that attendance should henceforth be optional.

Everybody in Concord, as they watched Mr. Emerson swinging along the road in his old gray clothes, or marching with his valise, black-coated and silk-hatted, to the railroad station for a lecture trip, knew that he had a good body. He was a rapid and tireless walker. Even at twenty, when his health was not yet established, he could do his forty miles a day without difficulty. All his life, he passed many hours of each day out of doors. He bought a rifle for his trip to the Adirondacks with W. J. Stillman.[9] That was why Longfellow refused to go: "Someone will get shot." But neither man nor deer was the worse for Emerson's weapon. He was a good skater and an excellent swimmer. In the Arcadian simplicity of that vanished epoch, when Emerson and Thoreau, or Ellery Channing and Hawthorne came on a hot day to a tempting pond or river, they peeled off their clothes and jumped in, drying themselves on the bank in the sunshine like truant schoolboys. Concord, as Frank Sanborn used to assert, was "the land of hyperbole and humor." With horses and cows and garden tools Emerson was inept, even more so than Alcott; but while Alcott's experiments with manual labor "depressed his spirits even to tears," Emerson smiled at his own awkwardness and kept on. He made light of the very real hardships involved in his long lecturing journeys. Once he drove forty-eight miles in a buggy over corduroy roads in Michigan to keep a lecture engagement, and then drove twenty more before he slept. Twice he had to cross the frozen Mississippi on the ice. On returning from a lecture trip in the West in February 1865 he wrote in his *Journals*: " 'Twas tedious, the squalor and obstructions of travel; the advantage of their offers at Chicago made it necessary to go; in short, this dragging of a decorous old gentleman out of home and out of position to this juvenile career was tantamount to this,—'I'll bet you fifty dollars a day that you will not leave your library, and wade and ride and run and suffer all manner of indignities and stand up for an hour each night reading in a hall'; and I answered, 'I'll bet I will.' I do it and win the $900." He needed the money, for the Civil War had greatly reduced his income, and he was trying to send his son Edward through college.

Every one in Concord knew that the simplicity and loveableness of Mr. Emerson's character was peculiarly manifest in his home. His second marriage, to Miss Lydia Jackson of Plymouth, was a perfect one. They changed her name, at his request, to Lydian Emerson, for euphony, but his own symbolical name for her was "mine Asia," a curious illustration of that fascination for the East which Emerson had felt from boyhood, and which he expressed in a youthful poem entitled "Asia," which

has never been printed. Mrs. Emerson was indeed
a woman of warm, opulent nature, endowed with
humor and patience. She did not write poetry, like
Ellen Tucker; she lived it. There is little about her
in print, as yet; and I hope there will never be
much. But those who know how to read between the
lines of her husband's *Journals* will remember what
he wrote there on June 11, 1840: "I finish this
morning transcribing my old essay on Love, but I
see well its inadequateness. I, cold because I am
hot,—cold at the surface only as a sort of guard
and compensation for the blind tenderness of the
core,—have much more experience than I have
written there, more than I will, more than I can
write. In silence we must wrap much of our life,
because it is too fine for speech, because also we
cannot explain it to others, and because somewhat
we cannot yet understand."

Emerson's mother, a gentle old lady, lived in the
front chamber over his study until her death in
1853. No description of her could be more vivid
than the note which her son wrote to his friend
S. G. Ward:[10] (November 22, 1853) "My little
household is grown much less by the loss of my
Mother. She was born to live. She lived eighty-four
years, yet not a day too long, and died suddenly
and unexpectedly at the last. She was born a subject of King George, and was bred in the Church
of England, and though she had lived through the
whole existence of this nation, and was tied all
round to later things, English traditions and courte-

sies and the Book of Common Prayer clung to her
in her age, and, had it been practicable, it would
have seemed more fit to have chanted the Liturgy
over her, and buried her in her father's tomb under
Trinity Church."

Serene as was the ordinary life of that household,
it would not have been normally human without
its sharp bereavements. Charles Emerson, one of
its inmates, who was betrothed to Elizabeth Hoar
and had expected to bring his bride to his brother's
roof, died in 1836. Edward had died in Porto Rico
two years earlier. Both of these young men had
extraordinary talent. Making every allowance for
family pride and affection, and remembering the
New England contrariness which still asserts that
John Holmes was more clever than his brother
Oliver Wendell, and Ezekiel Webster a better
lawyer than his brother Daniel, it remains true that
in 1836 both Edward and Charles Emerson were
ranked above Waldo, and their loss seemed irre-
parable. Then came, in 1842, the sudden death of
Emerson's first-born son. Those who recall the final
lines of the father's "Threnody" will know that he
found ultimately some measure of consolation, but
for two years after the event he suffered unhealed
agonies of sorrow, and the last words he uttered, as
he lay dying, forty years later, were these: "Oh,
that beautiful boy!" No one who has read Emerson's intimate and as yet unpublished correspondence can accept the superficial, but often repeated
opinion that this man never ate his bread with tears.

But work and love and the laughter of other children in the house came to his relief. One may say of Mr. and Mrs. Emerson what Cromwell said of his Ironsides: "They were never beaten." It is true that, compared with most of their neighbors, they had financial independence. A legacy from Ellen Tucker yielded about $1200 a year. Lectures, often at the rate of $10 apiece and very rarely exceeding $50, brought in $800 or $1000 more in average years. The income from Emerson's books was negligible until after the Civil War. But they lived in comfort, made constant private benefactions, and exercised a continuous hospitality. How Mrs. Emerson managed it is a secret that died with the generations which added to the Ten Commandments these other three: "Eat it up!" "Wear it out!" "Make it do!"

The guests of that friendly rooftree were of every conceivable variety. Some of them were mere "devastators of the day"; some, like Margaret Fuller, and the homeless Alcotts, stayed for weeks, and Emerson actually invited Thomas and Jane Carlyle to come over and share his home. Sometimes the guests were only mildly insane, like the Englishmen Lane and Wright; or they might be intermittently insane like Jones Very; or men of one idea, like Garrison and John Brown and Walt Whitman; or men of too many ideas, like Theodore Parker and Charles Sumner. In Hawthorne's preface to his *Mosses from an Old Manse* there is a matchless description of these strange visionaries and theo-

rists. Hundreds of sufferers from maladjustment
and spiritual depression came to Emerson for coun-
sel, as men and women at a later period went to
Dr. Weir Mitchell or to Dr. Riggs. Hundreds
more,—students, teachers, clergymen, journalists,
reformers,—wrote him long letters asking for ad-
vice. The Emerson house was a cure of souls,—
except that many of those souls were incurable. In
the jargon of hospital nurses at the present day,
they "went mental."

How did Emerson, amid these constant interrup-
tions and solicitudes, keep his sanity and produce
his twenty-two volumes? The answer is partly this:
the long, inviolable mornings in his study. Often
he was there by six o'clock, after a sound sleep and
a good breakfast, including two cups of coffee and—
it must be owned—a piece of pie; and there he
stayed—writing and thinking and writing again—
for some six hours. Sometimes he came back in the
afternoon, for two or three hours more. Such details
are prosaic; but the fact is that Emerson said so
much about his sauntering and writing "Whim"
over his door post that some persons are still
tempted to think of him as a day-dreamer and spiritual tramp. Certainly he could saunter in the long
Concord afternoons and be almost as whimsical as
Ellery Channing. But no mere saunterer could edit
the *Dial*—in the days when each issue of a maga-
azine meant hundreds of letters written by hand.
No saunterer could write the scholarly introduction
to Professor Goodwin's new edition of Plutarch's

Morals, and prepare those masterly addresses in the fields of biography, history and politics. Emerson was a very versatile and accomplished man of letters, but like most of the twenty-volume men, he had learned the Anthony Trollope trick of sitting in one's chair until the day's stint is finished,—and taking the gallop or the stroll afterwards.

V

But Emerson's life, as his Concord neighbors saw it—and in this chapter we have been trying to see it through their eyes—seemed to be spent in leaving the quiet friendly white house on the outskirts of the village, and in returning to it. He climbed into his chaise and drove placidly by the turnpike to Cambridge for those Phi Beta Kappa and Divinity School addresses which shook down the ancient walls of convention and revealed to his youthful hearers a new universe of thought and feeling. Then he climbed quietly into the chaise with Mrs. Emerson and drove back. From the white house he departed for England in 1847, leaving Henry Thoreau to stand valiant guard over his wife and babies, and after his round of English lectures and his social triumphs and his visit to Paris,—then in the throes of the Revolution of 1848,—back he came to his own rooftree once more, to spin his fairy web of thoughts. On the last Saturday of each month, after 1857, he took the train for the dinner of his beloved Saturday Club in Boston, where he sat silent, very often, smoking an excellent cigar, and smiling at the wit of Holmes and Agassiz and Lowell; then back again, by the very last train, to Concord. Society and Solitude; that was the alternation, that the Law.

Forever leaving,—for Chicago, for Washington, for San Francisco, for Egypt in his old age; and forever coming back to his books, to his favorite prints, to "mine Asia" and the children. Towards the end, after the last lecture had been given, he sat tranquilly in his study, his memory almost gone. I like that story of Swift in his sad old age, picking up *The Tale of a Tub*, looking through it as if it had been written by a stranger, and then exclaiming "Good God, what a genius I had when I wrote that book!" But I like still better the story of the aged Emerson, taking down his own *Essays* from the shelves, having forgotten all about them, and after reading awhile, saying to his daughter Ellen with a smile: "Why, those things are really very good!"

Only one short journey more remained, to the shadow of the pine trees in Sleepy Hollow, where, nearly thirty years earlier, in his address at the consecration of the cemetery, he had ended with the words: "Our dissatisfaction with any other solution is the blazing evidence of immortality."

As I reflect upon Emerson's life in Concord as he earned and shared his daily bread, I confess that I sometimes forget that he was a thinker and writer at all. I see only the great gentleman. Many of us, possibly, have that experience when we think about

Robert E. Lee. We know all about the argument for
secession and Lee's campaigns. Perhaps the Union
was worth saving; perhaps not; we forget. For there
sits Lee astride his grey horse Traveller, and—win-
ning or losing—what a gentleman!

It may be that in such moods we see the person
more truly than when we try to grasp him through
the mind. And I think it was in such a moment
of recognition that Oliver Wendell Holmes, who
had known Emerson for fifty years, closed his book
about him with the words to which all our new
twentieth century knowledge of Emerson can add
nothing: "If He who knew what was in man had
wandered from door to door in New England as of
old in Palestine, we can well believe that one of
the thresholds which 'these blessed feet' would have
crossed, to hallow and receive its welcome, would
have been that of the lovely and quiet home of
Emerson."

CHAPTER THREE

THE MYSTIC AND POET

"I am, like you, a seeker of the perfect and admirable Good. My creed is very simple, that Goodness is the only Reality, that to Goodness alone can we trust, to that we may trust all and always; beautiful and blessed and blessing is it, even though it should seem to slay me.

"Beyond this, I have no knowledge, no intelligence of methods; I know no steps, no degrees, no favorite means, no detached rules. Itself is gate and road and leader and march. Only trust it, be of it, be it, and it shall be well with us forever."

Letter of Emerson to an unknown correspondent,
July 3, 1841.

I

LET us now look at the other side of Emerson's face. No one who knew him in his lifetime, and no one today who turns the pages of his earliest *Journals* or glances at his first book, the *Nature* volume of 1836, has ever doubted his idealism or denied that this idealism is strongly colored by mysticism. He was a man of many gifts, and of manifold intellectual interests and practical activities, but his mystical tendencies were innate. If he had never been educated beyond the primary school, had never read Plato and Plotinus, St. Augustine and George Fox and Coleridge, he would still have been a mystic by nature, like countless illiterate men and women in all ages and of every race. "All

mystics," wrote Saint-Martin in the eighteenth century, "speak the same language and come from the
same country." But the language is not necessarily
that of books. The men and women who seek a
direct way to God, who are characterized by their
"intimate consciousness of the Divine Presence," are
often under-vocabularied; and even those who are
eloquent find that the experience which they wish to
describe is ineffable. The fact that Emerson happened to be well educated, and that all the influences surrounding his early life and his professional
studies tended to emphasize the significance of
philosophy and religion, are secondary influences
confirming, but not originating, the natural bent of
his mind.

He belonged, it will be admitted, to that group
which William James used to call the "healthy-
minded" mystics, a group which has been carefully
described by Rufus Jones,[1] Evelyn Underhill,[2] Dean
Inge,[3] and many other students of the psychology
and history of mysticism. Like all the mystics of
this group, and like many idealists who would prefer not to be labelled as mystics, the youthful Emerson discovered that for him, at least, Intuition,
rather than the processes of dialectics, was the most
direct way of apprehending Reality. He did not live
long enough to read in Bergson that the "analytical
faculties can give us no realities," but he had
already, at the age of twenty, written in his diary
that "the highest species of reasoning upon divine
subjects is rather the fruit of a sort of moral im-

agination, than of the 'Reasoning Machines,' such
as Locke and Clarke and David Hume."[4] He wrote
in Florida to his brother Edward: "Much of what
we learn, and to the highest purposes, of life is
caught in moments, and rather by a sublime instinct
than by modes which can be explained in detail."[5]
That is the doctrine of the "ecstatic moment,"
familiar to every student of mysticism. "My mind,"
wrote St. Augustine, "with the flash of one hurried
glance, attained to the vision of That Which Is."
(*Conf.*, Bk. VII, xvii.) The vivacious Meister Eckhart affirmed, perhaps less credibly: "In one quarter
of an hour I saw and knew more than if I had been
many years together at an University."

In Boston, as a young minister, Emerson writes
in his *Journal* (February 10, 1830): "Is there not
the sublime always in religion? I go down to the
vestry and I find a few plain men and women there,
come together not to eat or drink, or get money, or
mirth, but drawn by a great thought. Come thither
to conceive and form a connection with an infinite
Person. I thought it was sublime, and not mean, as
others suppose." It is a homely setting, this shabby
vestry of the North End Church, but "to conceive
and form a connection with an infinite Person," does
not that imply what the mystics call their doctrine
of "Transcendence"? See it in an even more homely
setting, as described by George Fox in a passage
that has become one of the classics of English prose:
"One morning, as I was sitting by the fire, a great
cloud came over me, and a temptation beset me,

and I sate still. And it was said, All things come by nature; and the Elements and Stars came over me, so that I was in a moment quite clouded with it; but, inasmuch as I sate still and said nothing, the people of the house perceived nothing. And as I sate still under it and let it alone, a living hope rose in me, and a true voice arose in me which cried: There is a living God who made all things. And immediately the cloud and temptation vanished away, and the life rose over it all, and my heart was glad, and I praised the living God."[6]

Here the doctrine of Transcendence passes over, very naturally, into the doctrine of Immanence. If there be a living God who made all things, is He not in everything that He has made? The classic statement of the Divine Immanence is of course St. Paul's: "In Him we live and move and have our being." But does He also live in wood and stone, in fire and water, in beast and bird? Eckhart[7] and St. Francis were very sure of it, as were Blake and Whitman and all the so-called "Cosmic Consciousness" men. Emerson's tentative grapplings with this doctrine, as revealed in his *Journals*, show that he came to it at first with some hesitation. In the field of morals, indeed, he could accept it. He wrote in 1830 (*Journals*, II, 317): "No man addicted to chemistry ever discovered a salt, or an acid, which he thought divine, never discovered a law which he thought God. No man devoted to literary criticism ever imagined that any of the thoughts that formed his study was God. But the man who cultivated the moral powers, ascended to a thought, and said *This is God*. The faith is the evidence." A few days later he is quoting Goethe (*Journals*, II, 330): "In works of art, there is much that is traditional; the works of nature are ever *a freshly uttered word of God*." In 1832, in some meditations on astronomy, he notes (*Journals*, II, 491): "The Sermon on the Mount must be true throughout all the space which the eye sees and the brain imagines." And by the summer of 1834 he takes the plunge into Immanence as recklessly as Blake or Whitman (*Journals*, III, 321): "What is there of the divine in a load of bricks? What is there of the divine in a barber's shop? . . . Much. All."

No wonder that four years later, in the Divinity School Address, he described the religious sentiment as "mountain air," as "myrrh and storax, and chlorine and rosemary" (to the disgust of Professors Alexander and Dod of Princeton!) and prophesied that the new Teacher "shall see the identity of the law of gravitation with purity of heart; and shall show that the Ought, that Duty, is one thing with Science, with Beauty and with Joy."

To the unilluminated intelligence, this looks marvellously like a "confusion of the *genres*." But was not William Blake stubbornly right when he declared "As a man is, so he sees"? And the Emerson who voiced his mystical raptures in the 1830's was the same Emerson who, returning from Europe at the age of seventy, kept pulling out his pocket compass with the naïve delight of a child, excusing himself to the disillusioned C. E. Norton, his fellow passenger, by saying: "I like to hold the visible god in my hand."[8] As a man is, so he sees.

II

Emerson's inborn capacity for certain states of the mystical consciousness was doubtless confirmed by some of the books which became his lifelong companions. Lovers of Charles Lamb will recall the passage in which he describes the youthful Coleridge at Christ's Hospital, unfolding in his "deep and sweet intonations, the mysteries of Iamblichus or Plotinus." Now Aunt Mary Moody Emerson,[9] with less sweet intonations, perhaps, could and did unfold Iamblichus and Plotinus to her favorite nephew. It was she, very probably, who first put him on the track of De Gérando's *Histoire Comparée des Systèmes de Philosophie*, an excellent handbook explaining the outlines of Oriental and Greek philosophy. He mastered it thoroughly, made long excerpts for his diary, and the reader of Emerson who turns today to Gérando's forgotten pages on Anaxagoras, Pythagoras and Heraclitus will recognize how deeply they affected the boy's vocabulary and mode of thought. While still a college student he found, like Coleridge before him, that Cudworth's *True Intellectual System of the Universe,*—a vast compilation by a Cambridge Platonist of the seventeenth century,—contained fascinating citations from Plato and other Greek philosophers. He

caught the infection, and began to read Plato for
himself, at first laboriously in the Greek, then in a
French translation, then, after a little, in the translation by Thomas Taylor (1758-1835), the enthu-
siastic and eccentric scholar, translator of both
Aristotle and Plato, who was so fascinated by Neo-
Platonism that he gave a Neo-Platonic coloring to
the doctrines of Plato himself. Late in Emerson's
life, Professor Jowett sent him his translation of
Plato, to Emerson's delight, but throughout his
early manhood he drank Plato's doctrine out of
Thomas Taylor's Neo-Platonic cup. Perhaps this
fact is not really so important as it seems to special
students; the chief thing is that he discovered Plato,
even though subtly transformed; for no really first-
rate man—except Benjamin Franklin!—ever read
Plato and was quite the same person afterward. That
was a great day in a man's life, Emerson once told
a schoolboy from Andover, when he first read the
Symposium.

To the young Puritan mystic, these first glimpses
of the peaks and cloudland of Greek thought were
an intoxication of the spirit. As in some divine
dance about the principle of all things—to borrow
a phrase from Plotinus—he perceived the balanced
movement of the eternal forces: the flux of change,
and the unchanging Absolute; matter and Spirit;
microcosm and macrocosm; time and eternity; the
many and the One; the triad of body, soul and
spirit, and the other trinity of the True, the Beau-

tiful, and the Good,—three coordinated manifestations of the One Reality.

When he came in later years to write his lecture on Plato, he still felt the spell. "Plato is philosophy, and philosophy, Plato." This is of course the graceful hyperbole of a lecturer, and his chapter on Plato is surely not one of Emerson's best, even though it contains his matchless portrait of Socrates. Yet he makes one remark about Plato which suggests curiously his own spiritual problem, namely, the attempt to balance Asia with Europe: the "Ocean of love and power" in the East, with the instinct of Culture—the cry "Yet all things are knowable" of the West. The young Emerson certainly possessed Spinoza's *amor intellectualis Dei;* he loved God with all his mind; and Plato helped him to define and to consider, to realize that the eternal values are knowable.

Yet on the more purely mystical side of his nature, he owed more to Plotinus than to Plato. It is one of the most singular facts in literary history, the influence exerted upon Emerson by an Egyptian-born wandering lecturer of the third century, of unknown race, who first learned philosophy from a baggage-carrier, taught in Alexandria and in Rome, and died in Campania, after finally writing out some of his discourses through the urgency of his pupil and biographer Porphyry. Plotinus wrote in a crabbed and difficult Greek. The last and greatest of the Alexandrine Neo-Platonists, his *Enneads* sum up the results of seven hundred years of speculation about the Platonic philosophy. Their influence upon Christian theology has been profound, and has never been so generally recognized as in the twentieth century. Yet there was no translation of Plotinus into English until Taylor published those volumes of selections which fell into Emerson's hands. Emerson seems to have reread them in at least eighteen different years of his life.[10] Their influence is traceable in many of his finest essays, in his theories of poetry, and in poem after poem. The motto for the first edition of *Nature* was chosen from Plotinus, and in the well known quatrain of his poem "Song of Nature" Emerson puts Plotinus into company with Jesus, Shakespeare and Plato:

> "One in a Judean manger,
>   And one by Avon's stream,
>   One over against the mouths of Nile,
>   And one in the Academe."

There is no occultism and nothing pathological in the mysticism of Plotinus. "All life," he says, "is a kind of spiritual vision." How much Orientalism may have entered into his interpretations of Plato is a matter on which modern scholars differ. Alexandria, as a cosmopolitan city of the Near East, was certainly swept in the third century by many currents of Oriental thought, and Plotinus himself is known to have journeyed into Mesopotamia. But to Emerson, whose knowledge of Neo-Platonism was based on Taylor's translations of selections, the Eastern influence seemed very strong. Dr. F. I. Carpenter, whose chapter on Neo-Platonism in his

Emerson and Asia gives an admirable survey of the subject, quotes Emerson as saying late in life to the Harvard students in his course on philosophy: "When Orientalism in Alexandria found the Platonists, a new school was produced. The sternness of the Greek school, feeling its way from argument to argument, met and combined with the beauty of Orientalism. Plotinus, Proclus, Porphyry and Iamblichus were the apostles of the new philosophy."[11]

Rightly or wrongly, that was Emerson's lifelong view. He loved what he called "the calm and grand air" of Plotinus; the stress upon intuition, upon the direct perceptions of the mystical experience; the doctrine of the journey of the soul of man toward the Great Soul, the World Soul; the mysterious efficacy of lonely contemplation; the faith that "nothing that truly is can ever perish." St. Augustine, who was converted to Neo-Platonism before he was converted to Christianity, ultimately found the philosophy of Plotinus lacking in the consciousness of sin, of alienation from God. It took no reckoning of the doctrine of vicarious suffering, of the Incarnation. Indeed the whole object of the mystic quest is to Plotinus, as Dean Inge has said, "a state and not a person. At no point in the ascent is God conceived as a Person over against our own personality. . . . The ineffable Godhead above God is of course supra-personal."[12]

Emerson recognized all this, of course, but he was not troubled by it. If it affected his own theological thought at all, it was probably a confirmation of a

drift—or, if one prefers, a coincidence with a blind
spot—in his own mind. What he admired in Plotinus
was the tone of spiritual elevation. He liked to go
up in that kind of airplane, without trying to make
any accurate topographical map of the receding
actual human landscape. Without Neo-Platonism
we should scarcely have had the essay on the "Over-
Soul" or the poem on the "World Soul" and many
another haunting passage in Emerson's prose and
verse.

A single illustration must here suffice. He found
in Taylor's translation of Plotinus this sentence:
"This, therefore, is the life of the Gods, and of
divine and happy men; a liberation from all terrene
concerns, a life unaccompanied with human pleas-
ures, and a flight of the alone to the alone." He
never forgot the last clause. He quotes it once—
perhaps more than once—in his letters. There is an
echo of it in the essay on the "Over-Soul": "the soul
gives itself, alone, original and pure, to the Lonely,
Original and Pure." Finally it appears twice, like
an overture and finale in the entrancing closing
paragraph of that essay on "Illusions" which com-
pletes his ripest book, *The Conduct of Life*: "There
is no chance and no anarchy in the universe. All is
system and gradation. Every god is there sitting in
his sphere. The young mortal enters the hall of the
firmament; there is he alone with them alone, they
pouring on him benedictions and gifts, and beckon-
ing him up to their thrones. On the instant, and in-
cessantly, fall snowstorms of illusions. He fancies

himself in a vast crowd which sways this way and
that and whose movement and doings he must obey:
he fancies himself poor, orphaned, insignificant. The
mad crowd drives hither and thither, now furiously
commanding this thing to be done, now that. What
is he that he should resist their will and think or act
for himself? Every moment new changes and new
showers of deceptions to baffle and distract him.
And when, by and by, for an instant, the air clears
and the cloud lifts a little, there are the gods still
sitting around him on their thrones,—they alone with
him alone."

III

It would be a very partial view of Emerson, however, if he were to be considered merely as one rapt in
high and cold meditations on the supremacy of the
moral laws of the universe. As a matter of fact,
although his biographers have said little about it, he
was deeply versed in the books of the distinctively
Christian mystics. He was a reader of St. Augustine's
Confessions and of *The Imitation of Christ*. Catholic
dogma did not interest him, though from boyhood he
had debated with his Aunt Mary the Augustinian
theology, as presented in the specific form of Calvinism. He remarked in his essay on "Character" that he
considered "the whole science of theology of great
uncertainty, and resting very much on the opinions of
who may chance to be the leading doctors of Oxford
or Edinburgh, of Princeton or Cambridge, today."
But with every genuine religious experience he was

sympathetic, and from the time of his visit to Sicilian churches he was responsive to the beauty of symbol and ritual. In a letter to Margaret Fuller, dated from Baltimore in January 1843, he gives a charming picture of a New England Puritan on a moral holiday:

"This morning I went to the Cathedral to hear mass with much content. . . . The chanting priest, the pictured walls, the lighted altar, the surpliced boys, the swinging censer every whiff of which I inhaled, brought all Rome again to mind. And Rome can swell so far! It is a dear old church,— the Roman, I mean, —and today I detest the Unitarians and Martin Luther and all the parliament of Barebones."[13]

Emerson loved the writings of seventeenth century Churchmen like George Herbert and Jeremy Taylor. He knew Bunyan, as he knew Milton, by heart. He found in Sir Thomas Browne's *Urn Burial* and *Religio Medici* not only a deeply devotional spirit, but the doctrine, always congenial to Emerson, of "signatures" and "correspondences": "In this mass of nature there is a set of things that carry in their front, though not in capital letters, yet in stenography, and short characters, something of divinity. . . . This visible world is but a picture of the invisible, wherein as in a portrait, things are not truly, but in equivocal shapes, and as they counterfeit some real substance in that invisible fabric." He recommended to his friends a tenderly devotional volume by a young Scotchman of the late eighteenth century, Scougal's *Life of God in the Soul of Man*. He knew George Fox's *Journal* well, and indeed lectured on Fox in one of his early

Boston courses. He was familiar with the writings of Jacob Boehme and of William Penn. Through his friend Sampson Reed,[14] a young Boston druggist, who wrote a stimulating little book called *The Growth of the Mind*, he became greatly interested in Swedenborg. In his *Representative Men*, it was Swedenborg who was chosen to represent the whole tribe of the mystics. Dr. Clarence Hotson,[15] who has recently made an exhaustive study of Emerson's relations with Swedenborgian thought, believes that he owed far more to Swedenborg than he ever confessed. But he certainly confessed indebtedness enough, and though he seems to have wearied at last of Swedenborgianism, he kept up an intimacy with Swedenborgian friends like Reed and Wilkinson and the elder Henry James. The whole experience with the Swedish visionary and his followers, was, if nothing more, a long gymnastic in mysticism.

To Dante, greatest of the Christian mystics, there are references scattered through Emerson's *Works* and *Journals*, but they are disappointing, save in their acknowledgment of Dante's power over words. Emerson thought Dante a "prodigy," as he well might, but he did not find in him "reason or illumination and that essence we were looking for."[16] He liked the *Vita Nuova*, but his dislike for the *Inferno* was intense, and perhaps he never went on to the *Paradiso*. Certainly he never discovered what *The Divine Comedy* was all about.

Of all the types of Western religious mysticism that Emerson encountered, the followers of the inner light were really the most congenial. His own words to David Greene Haskins are well known: "I believe I am more of a Quaker than anything else. I believe in the still small voice, and that voice is Christ within us." Nothing needs to be added to this. Yet one may be pardoned the conjecture that if any twentieth century books are allowed in those heavenly places which the spirit of Emerson now inhabits, no book could afford him a keener delight than the Quaker Professor Eddington's lecture before the London Society of Friends in 1929 on *Science and the Unseen World*. On the last page he might read: "If our so-called facts [of Science] are changing shadows, they are shadows cast by the light of constant truth. . . . We are repelled by that confident theological doctrine which has settled for all generations just how the spiritual world is worked; but we need not turn aside from the measure of light that comes into our experience showing us a Way through the unseen world." I think he might even prefer this book to his worn copy of Plotinus.

IV

Allusion has already been made to that specific mode of mystical thought known as Transcendentalism. It forms an essential chapter in the development of American literature, and special students, like O. B. Frothingham[17] and G. W. Cooke[18] of the older generation, and Goddard[19] and Riley[20] and others in our day, have made the general movement clearly understandable. The story need not be retold here. Yet there is one aspect of Emerson's connection with it that must be kept in mind by readers of the more mystical passages of his prose and verse. It is this: that the new vocabulary adopted for a while by the Transcendentalists gave them no essentially new experiences or points of view, although it did afford them a confirmation of their previous suspicions or intuitions, and granted to the hitherto tongue-tied the comfort of a common language. When I was a small boy I resolved with two or three companions to "name all the birds without a gun,"—none of us at that age being allowed to have guns,—and furthermore to name all the birds in Latin. A robin would alight cautiously upon the lawn. We whispered with boyish gravity: "A *turdus migratorius*!" To our fathers and mothers it was nothing but a robin, but we knew in our hearts that it was something more than that: it was a *turdus migratorius*!

I hope I am not pressing a too irreverent analogy if I now quote a letter written by Emerson to his brother Edward in 1834: "Do you draw the distinction of Milton, Coleridge and the Germans between Reason and Understanding? I think it a philosophy itself, and, like all truth, very practical. Reason is the highest faculty of the soul, what we mean often by the soul itself; it never *reasons*, never proves; it simply perceives, it is vision. The Understanding toils all the time, compares, contrives, adds, argues; near-sighted, but strong-sighted, dwelling in the present, the expedient, the customary."[21]

A little earlier than this Emerson had tried in his Notebook to reconcile the new terminology of Transcendentalism with the familiar language of the New Testament: "Jesus Christ was a minister of the pure Reason. The beatitudes of the Sermon on the Mount are all utterances of the mind contemning the phenomenal world. . . . The Understanding can make nothing of it. 'Tis all nonsense. The Reason affirms its absolute verity. Various terms are employed to indicate the counteraction of the Reason and the Understanding, with more or less precision, according to the cultivation of the speaker. A clear perception of it is the key to all theology, and a theory of human life. St. Paul marks the distinction by the terms natural man and spiritual man. When Novalis says 'It is the instinct of the understanding to counteract the Reason' he only translates into a scientific formula the sentence of St. Paul, 'The Carnal mind is enmity against God.' "[22]

One other brief quotation from the *Journals* of May 1832 shows how carefully Emerson had been pondering this question of nomenclature: "To be at perfect agreement with a man of most opposite conclusions you have only to translate your language into his. The same thought which you call *God* in his nomenclature is called *Christ*. In the language of William Penn, moral sentiment is called *Christ*."

In our day the distinction between the "reason" and the "understanding,"—though it was not without a real psychological basis,—has become as old-fashioned as the once famous distinction between

"fancy" and "imagination." No one doubts that
there is a difference between facts as perceived by the
senses, and truths as perceived by what we agree to
call "the mind." Thoreau's lines on "Inspiration"
are still suggestive:

> "I hearing get, who had but ears,
>   And sight, who had but eyes before,
> I moments live, who lived but years,
>   And truth discern, who knew but learning's lore."

Rupert Brooke wrote lines very similar. But not
even a Coleridge could excite our contemporaries
by balancing the "reason" over against the "understanding." Our cards are marked differently, though
the old game goes on. Yet of all the American Transcendentalists, I think Emerson had the shrewdest
literary and social instinct for the changing fashions
of speech; and certainly, more than any of them, he
was capable of the rapture of discovering his own
thoughts and experiences under the disguise of
strange patterns of English speech, and even in the
dialects spoken by other mystics, far away and long
ago.

V

This capacity for perceiving fundamental like-
nesses beneath the external divergencies of language
and of epochs is peculiarly marked in his enthusiasm
for the mystical utterances of the Far East. It seems
a long flight from the banks of the Musquetaquid to
the banks of the Ganges, but if one had the right airplane, as Emerson did, and had already tested the air-

ports of Athens and Alexandria, the journey was simple enough, and later flights to Persia, Arabia and China were easy. Emerson began to read translations of Hindu literature at nineteen, but it was not until he was nearly forty that he felt the real fascination of the sacred books of the East. He now read eagerly in the *Vedas* and the *Bhagavat Gîta* and the *Vishnu Sarma*. Young Henry Thoreau seems to have preceded him in these studies, and together they began to write about them in the *Dial*. It will be remembered that when Alcott, Lane, and Wright came over from London in 1843 for their ill-starred community experiment at Fruitlands, near Concord, they brought a library of one thousand volumes, by far the richest collection of mystical writings then to be found in the United States.[23] When Fruitlands became bankrupt, many of these books passed into the hands of Thoreau, and at his death he bequeathed some of his Oriental volumes to Emerson.[24] Concord's claim to be the pioneer of American Oriental studies is indisputable.

The wisdom of the Brahmins can scarcely be said to have effected any real changes in the general structure of Emerson's thought. That had become fairly fixed by 1838. Nevertheless, he discovered in the Hindu writings, as he had already found in Neo-Platonism, a reinforcement of certain natural mystical tendencies in himself. He used the forms and phrases of Hindu mythology as freely as he had handled the terms of Platonism. His famous poem "Brahma," for instance, printed in the first number of the *Atlantic Monthly*, aroused as much bewildered discussion as Mr. Kipling's mystical story "They," some fifty years afterward. Scholars point out that "Brahma" is a paraphrase from the *Vishnu Purana* and the *Katha-Upanishad*, and they are able to prove it, line by line. Yet the theme of the poem,—"the absolute unity of the world"—had long been familiar to Emerson's mind. I can never read the elaborate analyses of Emerson's "sources" for this poem without remembering one of Dr. Edward Emerson's favorite stories: how a small girl, ordered to memorize one of Emerson's poems, chose, to her teacher's amazement, "Brahma," because, she said, "Some of them were hard, but this was so easy to understand; it just meant, *God everywhere*."

So with "Hamatreya," the poem on land-hunger, which begins so gallantly with the names of old Concord pioneers: "Bulkley, Hunt, Willard, Hosmer, Merriman, Flint." I loved that poem as a boy, though the title seemed queer, and when I came later to read Anglo-Saxon, I thought it the best example in modern English of the Anglo-Saxon gnomic verse, full of race and the soil and stark primitive passion of possession.[25] But when Emerson's *Journals* were published it became perfectly clear that "Hamatreya" was based on a single passage of the *Vishnu Purana*, and is really, as Dr. Carpenter shows, a Hindu dialogue between Vishnu and Maitreya.[26] Thomas Carlyle's mother remarked, when she finished her Tom's first book, the *Life of Schiller*: "I see that foreign people have much the same feelings as ourselves."

Exactly. As far as we know, Emerson coined the word
"Over-Soul," but he had the pleasure of discovering
that the Hindu philosophy had a precisely equivalent
term (*paramatman*) for the same conception. And so,
for that matter, had Pythagoras and Plato. One
group of scholars finds Emerson's later thought peculiarly indebted to the Hindu doctrine of Illusion
(*maia*); another group points out that he had already
found it in the Greeks; and students of his earliest
writings are aware that he had no need to find it any-
where save in himself! He liked the Hindu expression "The internal check," but this was only an
Eastern paraphrase of what Aunt Mary Moody had
discussed with him when he was a schoolboy. In
short, Emerson's study of Indian thought did not
make him over into a fatalist, any more than Edward
Fitz-Gerald was made a pessimist by translating
Omar. "It is He that hath made us, and not we ourselves," is the text graven upon Fitz-Gerald's tomb-
stone.

The Persian poets gave Emerson a peculiar delight. He wrote poems and essays about them, translated many poems from Baron Purgstall's German
translations, and appropriated the name of Saadi—
"the poet of joy"—as a sort of disguised name for
himself, a stalking horse under which he could shoot
the arrows of his own wit. He loved Hafiz also, and
all his metaphors about wine and roses. He adorned
his letters and *Journals* and lectures with gaily colored quotations from these old Persians, without, of
course, knowing any more Persian than Amy Lowell

knew of Chinese. In one of his finest poems, "Bacchus,"—which Thomas Bailey Aldrich, a most fastidious poet and critic, once told me he would rather
have written than any American poem,—Emerson
uses "wine," in the Hafiz fashion, as a symbol not
merely of spiritual freedom, but of existence itself,—
as Rabelais had done in the sixteenth century. But
here again the source-hunters do not agree, and Harrison,[27] for instance, finds the origin of Emerson's
poem, not in Hafiz, but in Proclus and Plotinus.

Perhaps we do not yet understand the psychology
of these literary disguises. Poets may be like children
in amateur theatricals, taking pride and pleasure in
strange rôles, and yet somehow more truly like themselves when in costume than in their ordinary dress.
May not a Yankee Puritan, in identifying himself
with Saadi or Ali or Merlin, really reveal himself as
more of a Yankee than ever? I confess that I sometimes find Emerson in his Persian singing robes a
trifle theatrical. Edwin Arlington Robinson, in "Mr.
Flood's Party," makes old Eben Flood, climbing the
hill in Tilbury Town on a moonlit night, put down
his jug in the road and solemnly invite himself to
have a drink:

> "And with an acquiescent quaver said
> 'Well, Mr. Flood, if you insist, I might.
> Only a very little, Mr. Flood—' ."

There you have the authentic note of Bacchus in
Yankee-land, and it may outlast Emerson's imper-
sonations of Saadi and Hafiz.

And indeed when Emerson in his later writings quotes the *Koran* and the Arabs and Confucius, do we really feel ourselves in Arabia and China, or is it, in part at least, the old Lyceum device of ranging far for fresh illustrations, of making large vague reference to what is distant and unknown, the charm of names and places that we cannot quite identify? Audiences and readers whose memories were saturated with Bible names, who had absorbed a varied Oriental literature without suspecting that it was either "Oriental" or "literature," but simply the veritable *Verba Dei*, were possibly more responsive to such stimuli than the readers of today. "The Kings came and fought by the waters of Megiddo": one feels sure that it was a great fight, but who, except an archaeologist, ever wanted to look up Megiddo on the map?

VI

In Emerson's verse, then, as well as in his prose, there is often an element of the far-fetched, the exotic; words and phrases that have a histrionic, even a hypnotic savor. But all this is decorative, rather than structural. Mystic though he was in certain deep instincts, he knew perfectly well what he was about. If, like Plato as he understood Plato, he attempted to reconcile the dreams of the East with the exact knowledge of the West, and if, as W. T. Harris[28] said long ago, "he goes farther than Plato towards the Orient, and his pendulum swings farther west into the Occident," his mind was nevertheless ballasted by one fundamental faith, the faith in Law. Whether he is standing in the Museum of the *Jardin des Plantes* thrilled by his sudden revelation of the variety in Nature, or dreaming with Heraclitus about the eternal flux, or writing in his *Journals* (February 1847) : "What is the oldest thing? A dimple or whirlpool in water. That is Genesis, Exodus and all," he is forever holding stubbornly to his central conviction that law rules everywhere, that "Ought, that Duty, is one thing with Science, with Beauty and with Joy."

It is true that some of Emerson's admirers, quoting the striking lines from his "Ode to W. H. Channing",—

> "There are two laws discrete,
> Not reconciled,—
> Law for man and law for thing ;"—

have built upon them an elaborate theory of the different planes of being,—a conception familiar to Neo-Platonism. There are dialectic values in this distinction, though Emerson in his "Ode" is using it simply to protest against the materialism of pro-slavery politics. But his characteristic attitude towards the apparent divergency between "Law for man" and "Law for thing" is clearly set forth in one of his unprinted manuscript notebooks: "Socrates says 'The laws below are sisters of the laws above.' So really are the material elements of close affinity to the moral elements. But they are not their cousins, they are themselves. They are the *same laws* acting on superior and inferior planes. On the lower plane it is called

Heat, on the higher *Love*. Whenever you enunciate a physical law, I hear in it a moral rule."[29]

There speaks the unmistakable Emerson. Had he not declared in his book on *Nature* that "the laws of moral nature answer to those of matter as face to face in a glass. . . . The axioms of physics translate the law of ethics"? His favorite term, both for the recognition of this law, and for the law itself, is the "moral sentiment." That phrase, as I have already said, is his trump card, which he plays at the end of every close game. Or, to vary the metaphor, Emerson is like a golfer with naturally beautiful form, but with a tendency to pull or slice his drive, so that he is frequently in the rough. Yet it is precisely here that he shows his true quality. He pulls out of his bag an old iron club stamped "M. S.," and no matter how bad the lie or how great the distance he pitches his second shot dead to the pin. I call it an old club because the phrase "moral sentiment" goes back to those eighteenth century English philosophers whom Emerson read in college. Dr. James Bonar[30] has just written a witty book, entitled *Moral Sense*, about the history of the phrase. To Shaftesbury, and especially to Hutcheson, the term "moral sense" was synonymous with the instinct for right and wrong, conceived as a special faculty. Hume combated this theory, as did Adam Smith in his *Theory of Moral Sentiments* (1759)—a book which is in Emerson's library—and finally the terrible giant of Königsberg dealt it an apparently mortal stroke. Today, says Dr. Bonar, "the theory of a moral sense is without a patron." Yet Dr. Channing still held to Hutcheson, and when Emerson occupied Channing's pulpit in May 1829 he took "Moral Sentiment" as his theme.

It is easy for a certain class of minds to dismiss Emerson's insistence upon "moral sentiment" as irrational mysticism, but his conception of a universal moral law is none the worse for its embodiment in an ancient phrase. Today the psychologists like to coin new words for their battles, but some of the most dangerous controversialists of the eighteenth century, like Voltaire and Jefferson, preferred phrases already worn smooth on the lips of men,—as the young David picked his deadly stone—the smoother, the deadlier—from the bed of the brook.

VII

Emerson's own estimate of his skill as a poet was extremely modest. "I, who am only an amateur poet,"—he wrote to Dr. Furness in 1844. In writing to Lydia Jackson, shortly before their marriage, he went more into detail: "I am born a poet,—of a low class without doubt, yet a poet. That is my nature and vocation. My singing, to be sure, is very husky, and is for the most part in prose. Still I am poet in the sense of a perceiver and dear lover of the harmonies that are in the soul and in matter, and specially of the harmonies between these and those."[31]

That last sentence, roughly translated, means that we are to expect in his verse much of the characteristic thought of his prose; and there will always be

some readers who discover the real Emerson in his
poetry, as there will always be others who prefer to
find their Emerson in his *Journals* or *Essays*. But
everyone knows that he was a lifelong lover of verse.
He rendered it in public readings, with singular
beauty. He published an anthology of his favorite
poems, entitled *Parnassus*. He wrote verse from boyhood, usually keeping a separate notebook for that
purpose. Like Thoreau, he often scribbled the first
draft of a poetical thought in rude blank verse, which
was afterward turned into rhyme or honest prose. The
prose draft of his rhymed poem "Two Rivers," for
instance, seems to many readers to possess a more
delicate harmony than the metrical version. Emerson printed some of his verse in the *Dial* and elsewhere, and in 1847 and 1867 published two slender
volumes which neither raised nor lowered his reputation in his own generation.

The *obiter dicta* on poetry uttered by this veteran
reader and writer are often memorable: "The great
poets are judged by the frame of mind they induce";
"It is not metres, but a metre-making argument, that
makes a poem"; "In poetry, tone: . . . the uncon-
trollable interior impulse which is the authentic mark
of a new poem, and which is unanalyzable, and
makes the merit of an ode of Collins, or Gray, or
Wordsworth, or Herbert or Byron,—and which is
felt in the pervading tone, rather than in brilliant
parts or lines"; and finally, at the very end of his
life, "The secret of poetry is never explained,—is always new. We have not got any farther than mere

wonder at the delicacy of the touch, and the eternity it inhabits"; these are sayings worthy of Coleridge or Keats.

It is true that the off-hand verdicts of his *Journals* upon the poets whom he happened to be reading were sometimes whimsical or shallow. If he failed to catch the virtue of Shelley or Aristophanes, it was no worse than his blindness to the talent of Jane Austen and of Dickens. But very often his judgment of new volumes of verse was keen. To take but a single instance, he caught by 1838 the "musky odor" of Tennyson's early verse; in 1851 he found in *In Memoriam* "the commonplaces of condolence among good Unitarians in the first week of mourning. The consummate skill of the versification is the sole merit"; but in 1872 he noted, "The only limit to the praise of Tennyson as a lyric poet is that he is alive. If he were an ancient, there would be none,"—a remark which might well be pondered by the twentieth century disparagers of Tennyson. What a pity that Emerson and Tennyson did not make their projected visit to Paris together in 1848, among "the French bullets" the thought of which amused Emerson, but made Tennyson nervous!

Emerson's formal essays on poetry and the poetic art,—such as "The Poet," "Poetry and Imagination," "Shakespeare, the Poet," and "Persian Poetry,"—while highly individual in their phrasing, present a curious blend of the theories of Platonism and the Persians, of Elizabethan and seventeenth century practice, and of conventional late eighteenth

century aesthetics, as modified by Coleridge, Wordsworth and Blake. In such matters Emerson was an
unashamed eclectic, and his enormously wide reading
in poetry furnished him with examples of the most
divergent theory and practice. In this field, as elsewhere, he has no theory to inculcate: he simply com-
municates an enthusiasm for poetry and interprets it
with an insight denied to the system-makers.

The excellencies and defects of Emerson's own
verse are so patent that schoolmasters deal with
them swiftly. Whether one opens his *Poems* with the
amused indifference of an undergraduate or with the
affectionate loyalty of long acquaintance, certain
superficial traits are clear. That exquisite choice of
the right word,—sometimes a surprising, daring
word,—which characterizes his prose style, often
sparkles in his verse. "The Sphinx is drowsy"; "Devastators of the day"; "She spired into a yellow
flame"; "His formidable innocence"; " Our sump-
tuous indigence"; "All the brags of plume and song."
Such words fairly crackle. He is a master likewise, at
times, of the full poetic phrase or line: "Voyager of
light and noon"; "April cold with dropping rain";
"The eternal sky, Full of light and of deity"; "The
vast skies fall, Dire and satirical"; "O tenderly the
haughty day Fills his blue urn with fire." Emerson
loves the tightly packed line as well as the master of
his youth, Alexander Pope: "He builded better than
he knew"; "And striving to be man, the worm
Mounts through all the spires of form"; "And music
pours on mortals Its beautiful disdain." Yet even

these are no better in their way than his countless
prose aphorisms, like "All the world loves a lover."

Some of the ringing lines of this cunning rhetorician are perhaps only oratory in disguise: "Things
are in the saddle And ride mankind"; "When half-
gods go, The gods arrive"; "fired the shot heard
round the world." His finest achievement in this
oratorical *genre* is the stanza of the "Boston Hymn"
read in Music Hall on January 1, 1863. His worried,
anxious audience had been waiting for hours for the
expected telegram from Washington telling them
that Lincoln had at last signed the Emancipation
Proclamation. Both Emerson and Lincoln had been
at times advocates of the policy of compensated
emancipation. But no orator ever caught his audience
more completely off-guard than did Emerson with
his unexpected climax:

> "Pay ransom to the owner
> And fill the bag to the brim.
> Who is the owner? The slave is owner,
> And ever was. Pay him."

That brought the crowd to its feet, shouting, in the
winter twilight.[32]

The present-day advocates of *poésie pure*, that is
to say, poetry unadulterated by any foreign substance, such as ethical content, are suspicious of
Emerson's patriotic verse, like the "Boston Hymn"
just mentioned, the "Concord Ode," and "Volun-
taries"—written in memory of fallen soldiers of the
Civil War. It is true that in all these poems, and in
Emerson's rhymed counsels of perfection for the in-

dividual, like "Fate," "Sursum Corda," "To J. W.,"
and "Give all to Love," there is an element of ethical
admonition and appeal. But so there is in Milton's
sonnets and in much of the most authentic poetry of
the English race. The critic who would cut out the
ethical, even the didactic, strain from English poetry
would succeed only in emasculating it.

It is obvious, however, that though Emerson was
undeniably an ethical teacher, he was by no means
invariably in the pulpit, either as prose-man or poet.
He could write purely objective poems about Nature,
sometimes merely descriptive like "The Snow Storm"
and the "Sea-Shore," and sometimes with the height-
ened lyric transport of "The Humble-Bee" and
"May-Day." Now and again there will be a group of
lines as detached from everyday reality, as haunting
in their unearthly cadence, as anything in Poe:

> "Subtle rhymes, with ruin rife,
> Murmur in the house of life,
> Sung by the Sisters as they spin;
> In perfect time and measure they
> Build and unbuild our echoing clay,
> As the two twilights of the day
> Fold us music-drunken in."[33]

Emerson frequently composed poetic meditations
based upon his chance experiences out of doors, like
"Each and All," "The Rhodora" and "The Tit-
mouse"; or upon growing old, as in "Terminus"; or
upon sharp bereavement, as in the "Dirge" over his
two brothers and the "Threnody" upon the death of
his son. In such poems there is little attempt to gen-

eralize or to enforce any doctrine. They are poems of
"occasion," in Goethe's sense of the word. It is true
that Matthew Arnold failed to understand "The Tit-
mouse," never having seen one and never having been
lost in the deep snow of the New England woods.
There is, by the way, a curious parallel to this poem
in one of Turgenev's *Poems in Prose*, called "We
Shall Still Fight On," written when Turgenev was
already suffering from his incurable disease of the
spine:

"What an insignificant trifle can sometimes put the whole
man back in tune!

Full of thought, I was walking one day along the highway.

Heavy forebodings oppressed my breast; melancholy
seized hold upon me.

I raised my head. . . . Before me, between two rows of
lofty poplars, the road stretched out into the distance.

Across it, across that same road, a whole little family of
sparrows was hopping, hopping boldly, amusingly, confi-
dently!

One of them in particular fairly set his wings akimbo,
thrusting out his crop, and twittering audaciously, as though
the very devil was no match for him! A conqueror—and
that is all there is to be said.

But in the meantime, high up in the sky, was soaring a
hawk who, possibly, was fated to devour that same conqueror.

I looked, laughed, shook myself—and the melancholy
thoughts instantly fled. I felt daring, courage, a desire for
life.

And let *my* hawk soar over *me* if he will. . . .

'We will still fight on, devil take it!' "

Now neither Turgenev nor Emerson is guilty of any exhortation to others. They report a private adventure of the soul.

Emerson is rich also in a sort of gnomic or wisdom verse, which in its mood is reflective rather than didactic, although we are free to apply the latent "morality"—as Chaucer says—if we will. "Letters," "Days," "The Problem," "Brahma" and "Hamatreya" belong here, as do "Merlin" and "Saadi,"—poems about poetry,—many verse mottoes and apothegms, and the "Initial, Daemonic, and Celestial Love," where Emerson starts with Plato, but finding the final grade rather difficult, shifts gears expertly into Plotinus.

VIII

At this point the Devil's Advocate, who is always present at these "Assizes of the Poets," is getting restless and insists upon being heard. He admits,—being a sensible fellow and not without literary taste,—that Emerson has many interesting and indeed valuable things to say. But he insists that most if not all of them could be said in prose. The Devil's Advocate agrees that Emerson possesses a remarkable instinct for the brilliant single word or the pregnant phrase, but he points out coolly that the loveliest fragments of stained glass do not make a window unless there is a pattern, a controlling design. Emerson is a marvellous ejaculator of poetic phrases, no doubt, but is he a true builder of the lofty rhyme; has he the architectonic gift and training? And even

as an artisan of the lesser units of verse-making, are
not his words frequently harsh, his stresses grotesque,
his rhymes abominable? Why could he not have employed a competent poetic secretary, like Christina
Rossetti, to put his thoughts into impeccable verse?

I grant,—continues the Devil's Advocate,—that
with good luck he may achieve a quatrain. The one
beginning "So nigh is grandeur to our dust" and that
other about " 'Tis man's perdition to be safe" are indeed "excellent,"—if I recall rightly the adjective
used by a Mr. Arnold, who has been frequently cited
as a witness in this Court. Yet does not Emerson show
a singular lack of sustained and symmetrical beauty?
Could he by any possibility follow a complicated
stanzaic pattern, or even turn out a respectable Pet-
rarchan sonnet? Is not the "fatal facility" of his
favorite octo-syllabic line really more fatal to him
than it was to Scott or Byron, inasmuch as Emerson
lacks utterly the narrative genius which held their
lines together? Why should he be so incoherent, so
wilful, so tantalizing? I believe he has read too much
Donne and Cowley and Crashaw, and not enough
Virgil and Dante. And yet for all his affectation of
humility, I suspect that when he is wearing his singing robes he is really arrogant, even—if I may be
pardoned the term—pontifical. In conclusion,—may
it please the Court,—I like this gentleman personally,
and have frequently been stimulated by his ideas,
even if he does come out of a queer epoch and from a
country as yet imperfectly civilized. But I can never
submit to seeing him enthroned in the hierarchy of the

great poets, or even beatified among the poets of the
second class. And what is worse, he seems to be smiling at me in this very moment, as if this were not an
extremely serious occasion! And with that, the
Devil's Advocate sits down.

Now there is no doubt that Emerson is smiling a
little,—with that baffling smile that always irritated
his opponents. Perhaps he is thinking of Ben Jonson's
remark about Shakespeare: "He wanted art." Or possibly he is thinking of his own dictum: "The great
poets are judged by the frame of mind they induce."
Let us take that sentence,—not as a mere rejoinder to
the Devil's Advocate, for he has been asserting some
indisputable truths,—but for a suggestion that an
appeal may be taken to the jurisdiction of another
court.

What, then, is the frame of mind induced in the
reader of such poems as the "Ode to Beauty," "Fore-
runners," "May-Day," "The Sphinx," "The World-
Soul," "Woodnotes," "Monadnock," "Bacchus," and
the second movement of the "Threnody"? In most of
these poems there are traces, no doubt, of faulty
drawing, unbalanced proportion, some obscurity and
a strangely syncopated music. They are all mystical
in their mood, built upon the perception of some endless Quest,—what the mystics call, in their various
dialects, the Journey, the Way, the Life. These
poems are profoundly spiritual, and to grasp their
full meaning requires a degree of spiritual divination
which few of us possess. And nevertheless, the man
who is least like Emerson in his mental habits and

range of perception can scarcely fail to become aware, in reading this group of poems, of certain truths about the world of appearance as related to the world of reality. He becomes conscious,—intimately and intensely conscious,—of beauty as it is revealed through the senses. The Wine of Being suffers "no savor of the earth to scape.'

"That I intoxicated,
And by the draught assimilated
May float at pleasure through all natures;

The bird-language rightly spell,
And that which roses say so well.

* * * * * *

Wine that is shed
Like the torrents of the sun
Up the horizon walls,
Or like the Atlantic streams, which run
When the South Sea calls.

* * * * * *

Winds of remembering
Of the ancient being blow,
And seeming-solid walls of use
Open and flow.

Pour, Bacchus, the remembering wine;
Retrieve the loss of me and mine!

* * * * * *

Refresh the faded tints,
Recut the aged prints,
And write my old adventures with the pen
Which on the first day drew,
Upon the tablets blue,
The dancing Pleiads and eternal men."

The sheer beauty of the visible world, which stings the senses and exalts or saddens the thinking mind, is according to Emerson an expression or symbol of the inner life of the universe. The symbols are transient:

"Somewhat not to be possessed
Somewhat not to be caressed,
No feet so fleet could ever find,
No perfect form could ever bind."

Yet the inner life endures, being in its nature endless.

"All the forms are fugitive
But the substances survive.
Ever fresh the broad creation,
A divine improvisation,
From the heart of God proceeds,
A single will, a million deeds.

The world is the ring of his spells
And the play of his miracles."

The chief miracle, to Emerson's view, is that "conscious Law," the "King of Kings," which ranges throughout the universe of matter and the swiftly altering civilizations of men. He believes that there is no real and final dualism, only temporary and apparent oppositions between different manifestations and phases of the one Law. Every dancing atom obeys it. Standing on the granite summit of Monadnock, we should perceive, if we were only sensitive enough:

"How the chemic eddies play,
Pole to pole, and what they say;
And that these gray crags

Not on crags are hung,
But beads are of a rosary
On prayer and music hung.

* * * * * *

For the world was built in order,
And the atoms march in tune."

And yet the mountain, Emerson believes, cannot "measure with man," though both are subject to the same Law. What are our towns and cities and railways but

"sailing foam-bells
Along Thought's causing stream"?

All the tangible phenomenon of civilization thus become types of

"The soul's pilgrimage and flight."

It is true that this pilgrimage of the soul cannot be adequately comprehended by our human intelligence; and in the *finale* of Emerson's "Threnody" there is a passage which reminds one of Tolstoi's injunction, in certain exigencies of life, to "stop thinking," because thought will not carry one through:

"When the scanty shores are full
With thought's perilous, whirling pool;
When frail Nature can no more,
Then the Spirit strikes the hour:
My servant Death, with solving rite,
Pours finite into infinite."

Yet this very infinitude is not one of Oriental quiescence, but a limitless Energy which pulses through the illusions of Space and Time. In Em-

erson's final vision, as in John Fox's by the kitchen
fire, "The Life rises over it all":

> "Not of adamant and gold
> Built he heaven stark and cold;
> No, but a nest of bending reeds,
> Flowering grass and scented weeds;
> Or like a traveller's fleeing tent,
> Or bow above the tempest bent;
> Built of tears and sacred flames,
> And virtue reaching to its aims;
> Built of furtherance and pursuing,
> Not of spent deeds, but of doing.
> Silent rushes the swift Lord
> Through ruined systems still restored,
> Broadsowing, bleak and void to bless,
> Plants with worlds the wilderness;
> Waters with tears of ancient sorrow
> Apples of Eden ripe tomorrow,
> House and tenant go to ground,
> Lost in God, in Godhead found."

According to the legend, Prometheus stole fire
from Heaven, and brought it down to earth hidden
in a hollow stalk of fennel. You would call a stalk
of fennel a very odd and ineffective receptacle for
the divine spark. But the poor frozen children of
men, we may imagine, cared little what it was that
contained the precious flame. They wanted fire,—
and the frame of mind that fire induced.

CHAPTER FOUR

REVALUATIONS

*"I do not judge men by anything they can do. Their
greatest deed is the impression they make on me. Some serene,
inactive men can do everything."*

Thoreau's *Journals.*

I

IT IS nearly fifty years ago that Matthew Arnold,
lecturing in America only two years after Emerson's death, declared that Emerson was not "a
great poet, a great writer, a great philosophy-maker";
and yet he pronounced Emerson's *Essays* "the most
important work done in prose" during the nineteenth
century. Arnold explained his paradox, as everyone
remembers, by calling Emerson "the friend and
aider of those who would live in the spirit," and
claiming that this is a "relation of even superior
importance" as compared with the work of "a great
poet, a great writer, a great philosophy-maker."

In the fourth decade of the twentieth century,
many of those literary valuations attempted in the
nineteenth century seem outmoded, perhaps more
outmoded than they really are. Fifty years in the
history of science bring startling changes. Fifty
years in the history of literature may mean very
little in the way of revaluation. A great book is not
a corner lot, whose value must be re-assessed from

year to year as the population shifts. Are we and
our friends of the present decade any better judges
of wisdom and beauty as revealed through words
than were Charles Lamb and his friends a hundred
years ago? Or Pope and his friends two hundred
years ago, or Ben Jonson and his friends a hundred
years earlier, or Erasmus and his friends a hundred
years earlier still? I cannot think that we are. The
perception of beauty and wisdom depends upon
the perceiver, and not upon mass opinion in the
market-place.

And nevertheless it is undeniable that time works
certain changes in our observation of what we call
timeless things. The scale of values, the apparent
impact of significant poets and prose-men upon the
mind, the apparatus and the methods of literary
measurement, are bound to shift a little as the generations pass. In my grandfather's time as an
undergraduate, Pope was still the man in poetry; in
my father's time it was Wordsworth; in mine it was
Tennyson and Browning; in my son's it was Kipling
and Masefield; and our grandchildren will certainly
make their own choices, irrespective of what the
critics say. Yet the reading men of each of those generations were perfectly aware that Virgil, let us say,
or Milton, was a greater artist than their own
literary hero of the hour. What is excellent is
permanent, however widespread be the conspiracy
to make us forget it. Nevertheless there are degrees
of excellence, specialized forms and functions of excellence, fitted to render peculiar service to human-

ity in one period rather than another. The special literary service performed by Petrarch, for example, or Goethe, or Walter Scott, is a unique contribution to the European culture of their day, and apparently could not be duplicated by men of equal gifts in any subsequent epoch, since the conditions of European civilization have so materially altered.

It is in this consideration of the temporary and local effectiveness of certain writers that one form of present-day disparagement of Emerson takes its rise. Admitting that he had something beautiful and valuable to say in the epoch of little red schoolhouses and country Lyceums and a general Age of Innocence, has not our present complicated and sophisticated American civilization passed beyond the need and the reach of such a voice as Emerson's? We may agree to honor him for his service to our fathers and grandfathers, as we honor a George Rogers Clark for exploring the Northwest; but now that there is no longer any frontier, there is no rôle left for a frontiersman. Give him a statue, of course, and a page in the *Dictionary of American Biography*, but he is no longer an actual factor in our whirling world of motor cars and radios and skyscrapers.

To illustrate this feeling that Emerson is now a mere relic of the Age of Innocence, I venture to quote three disillusioned graduates of Harvard. Charles Eliot Norton, writing to Lowell about Emerson's seventieth birthday, spent on shipboard, says wistfully: "He is the youngest man I know. [Norton himself was then forty-five.] . . . At times he made me internally impatient with his inveterate and fatalistic optimism; he admits no facts that bear against his philosophy,—a philosophy that has its rise in the pure atmosphere of the America before 1830."[1] Barrett Wendell, writing thirty years later, is equally convinced of Emerson's worldly ignorance: "In his effort to express truth, just as in his whole knowledge of life, he was limited by the national inexperience which throughout his time still protected New England."[2] And Henry Adams, the third member of this initiated and self-conscious group, in his *Education of Henry Adams* dismisses Emerson with the fatal word "naïf."[3]

Let us take a still more recent example of what is essentially the same criticism. Mr. James Truslow Adams, in an article in the *Atlantic* for October 1930, entitled "Emerson Re-Read," reports that the Emerson who stirred him at sixteen leaves him cold at fifty. Where is the trouble? It must be, Mr. Adams thinks, in the five volumes (out of twenty-two!) which he has just been re-reading, apparently for the first time since boyhood. And here, surely enough it is: "a fatally easy philosophy"; "aphorisms which stir the soul of the young and the not too thoughtful"; "a shallow optimism" which "fails us as we grow older and wiser"; "a culture a bit thin and puerile"; a man "lacking in depth and virility," who has never felt suffering, any more than America has yet felt suffering.

Mr. Adams, it is true, "would still have every youth read his Emerson,"—as he would, presumably, have every child taught to believe in Santa Claus. But "is it well," he asks, "that 'the outstanding figure in American letters' [a phrase which he has quoted from Paul Elmer More] should be one whose influence diminishes in proportion as the minds of his readers grow in strength, breadth and maturity? . . . Does any man of steadily growing character, wealth of experience and strength of mind find the significance and influence of Emerson for him growing as the years pass? . . . There is but one answer, I think, and that is negative. Unlike the truly great, the influence of Emerson shrinks for most of us as we ourselves develop." I am tempted, at this point, to remind the reader of the testimony of William James, already quoted: "Reading the whole of him [Emerson] over again continuously has made me feel his real greatness as I never did before." But perhaps William James—all unsuspected by his friends—lacked a "steadily growing character"!

This confession of Mr. Adams, like the passages already quoted from Norton and Wendell and Henry Adams, is unmistakably sincere. They all feel wiser than Emerson, but that discovery does not seem to bring them much happiness. They feel that they have been fooled. Like Truthful James and his friend William Nye, who, according to Bret Harte's poem, once played a disastrous game of euchre against a pensive and inexperienced Chinaman with long sleeves, they perceive that there is something wrong somewhere. And the trouble lies, they are sure, with Emerson, the "childlike and bland" Oriental, who "did not understand" the game of life, but managed somehow to cheat them.

I hazard the possibly rude query whether some of Emerson's critics may not really be more *naïf* than he! But it is childish to exchange epithets. The only way to discover the truth or falsity of Emerson's utterances is to read and re-read, with prosaic fidelity, everything that he wrote; to test its pertinence to American life by a thorough-going examination of the history of the United States during his lifetime and of the social, political and literary movements since his death; and finally to test the validity of his counsels to the individual by a dispassionate and unwearied comparison of them with other reports about human life that men have found significant. No such ambitious program has been attempted by any of Emerson's biographers and critics. It is not likely to be undertaken until a great deal of hitherto unprinted material has been published and assimilated. In the meantime one who has read Emerson with ever increasing delight since boyhood may be permitted to offer a few suggestions.

II

In the first place, the whole theory of our national inexperience, illustrated by the personal inexperience of Ralph Waldo Emerson, is a myth. His ancestors migrated to America three hundred years ago. They were competent Englishmen, with the experience of many centuries of civilization behind them. They brought with them long-tested institutions, and they had the resourcefulness to frame new institutions as these were needed. To imagine John Smith and John Winthrop and William Bradford as novices in human society is amusing. Neither were Franklin and Washington and Jefferson precisely babes in the woods. Mr. James Truslow Adams's admirable volumes on New England history reveal that an unworldly idealism was by no means the only stock-in-trade of the colonists. The legend of "a pure America" before 1830 was exploded by Henry Adams in his monumental *History of the United States during Jefferson's Administration.* The era in which Emerson grew to manhood,—the period of Jackson and John Quincy Adams and Clay and Van Buren,—while simple enough compared with ours in its economics and its manners, was far from being a simple-minded epoch. It was a turbulent, caustic, questioning, many-sided period. "Men were born," it was said, "with knives in their brain." To say that Emerson never suffered is to be strangely ignorant of his biography; to rebut the charge that America never suffered one has only to look at the face of Lincoln. More than half of the able-bodied men in Vermont volunteered for the Civil War. Virginia made an even heavier sacrifice. And even after the Union had been preserved, was there no cruelty and injustice in the vast industrial and commercial epoch that followed? And is there not cruelty and injustice and stupidity today, and widespread poverty and bitterness? Emerson's "optimism" is the optimism that would if possible transcend evil rather than merely deny its existence; it is an endeavor to find "some soul of goodness in things evil, would men observingly distil it out."

Let us linger for a moment in the field of politics, with which Emerson, like Whittier and Lowell and Whitman, felt such intimate concern. There are about seventy essays and sixty addresses and articles in Emerson's published works. Over twenty of these productions deal directly with American politics, to say nothing of his political verse, the countless political notes throughout the *Journals* and the constant political illustrations that appear in the *Essays*. How much of this material is still vital? Most of the specific issues on which Emerson spoke or wrote have long been settled, and what he said is chiefly of interest today as revealing his character and his mastery of prose style; but every now and then his comments fairly leap at you from the page, being as pertinent to our times as if written yesterday.

Among the closed issues, we may choose, as a single illustration, the subject of Slavery. Emerson lent his pulpit to an Anti-Slavery speaker in 1831, at a time when few if any Boston ministers would have dared to do it, but he never joined the sect of the Abolitionists, and many of them thought him lukewarm in the cause. It was not until his Concord speech of 1844, to celebrate the tenth anniversary of

Emancipation in the British West Indies, that he took an unequivocal stand. Young Henry Thoreau, by the way, secured the use of the Court House for this meeting, and rang the bell himself. It was now that Emerson confessed that in his solitary walks he had been oppressed by the thought of slavery in his own country, and declared that "the civility of no race can be perfect whilst another race is degraded." Yet it was not until after the passage of the Fugitive Slave Law that he grew hot: "There is infamy in the air. I have a new experience. I wake in the morning with a painful sensation, which I carry about all day, and which, when traced home, is the odious remembrance of that ignominy which has fallen on Massachusetts, which robs the landscape of beauty, and takes the sunshine out of every hour. . . . An immoral law makes it a man's duty to break it. . . . This is not meddling with other people's affairs: this is hindering other people from meddling with us. . . . You know that the Act of Congress of September 18, 1850, is a law which every one of you will break on the earliest occasion. . . . You have a law which no man can obey, or abet the obeying, without loss of self-respect and forfeiture of the name of gentleman."[4] In his private diary he had already written: *"I will not obey it, by God!"*[5]

His New York speech on the "Fugitive Slave Law," delivered on March 7, 1854, is one of the most magnificent invectives in the English language, marred only by a lack of charity,—perhaps it would be better to say with Mr. J. J. Chapman a positive "ferocity,"—toward Daniel Webster, who had died in 1852. We must pass over Emerson's speeches in Kansas, and on the assault upon Charles Sumner; on John Brown, on the death of Lincoln, on "American Civilization"—which Lincoln is thought to have heard on its first delivery in Washington in 1862,— and on "The Fortune of the Republic." No one can read these speeches today, and believe any longer in the queer legend that represents Emerson as a mere stroller in the Concord woods, a mere Platonic dreamer of supernal beauty. "When I see how much work is to be done,"—he had written to Carlyle in 1841,—"what room for a poet—for any spiritualist—in this great, intelligent, sensual and avaricious America, I lament my fumbling fingers and stammering tongue." But when the right hour struck, his fingers did not fumble and the tongue became a tongue of flame.

III

In turning to Emerson's political utterances on topics that are just now before the public, I must pass over what he said about international peace, and the short-sightedness of tariffs, and equal rights for women: "All my points would sooner be carried in the State if women voted." I choose rather, a few sentences from the essay on "Politics," published indeed in 1844, though the watermark seems to me to read unmistakably 1931.

"Republics abound in young civilians who believe that the laws make the city, that grave modifications

of the policy and modes of living and employments
of the population, that commerce, education and
religion may be voted in or out; and that any nonsense, though it were absurd, may be imposed on a
people if only you can get sufficient voices to make
it a law. But the wise know that foolish legislation
is a rope of sand which perishes in the twisting; that
the State must follow and not lead the character and
progress of the citizen; . . . and that the form of
government which prevails is the expression of what
cultivation exists in the population which permits
it. The law is only a memorandum."

Coming from a man who was born in the heyday
of Boston Federalism, that passage is singularly
Jeffersonian. Still more so are these sentences from
Emerson's "Speech on Affairs in Kansas": "I own
I have little esteem for governments. . . . I set the
private man first. He only who is able to stand alone
is qualified to be a citizen. Next to the private man,
I value the primary assembly, met to watch the
government and to correct it. . . . First, the
private citizen, then the primary assembly, and the
government last."

And yet, in the essay on "Politics," Emerson is
equally fair to Hamiltonianism, to the rights of property as well as to the rights of persons. "Property
will, year after year, write every statute that respects
property." Justly famous is his analysis of the align-
ment of American political parties: "Of the two
great parties which at this hour almost share the
nation between them, I should say that one has the

best cause, and the other contains the best men. The philosopher, the poet, or the religious man, will of course wish to cast his vote with the democrat, for free trade, for wide suffrage, for the abolition of legal cruelties in the penal code, and for facilitating in every manner the access of the young and the poor to the sources of wealth and power. But he can rarely accept the persons whom the so-called popular party propose to him. . . . The spirit of our American radicalism is destructive and aimless: it is not loving. . . . On the other side, the conservative party, composed of the most moderate, able and cultivated part of the population, is timid, and merely defensive of property. . . . From neither party, when in power, has the world any benefit to expect in science, art, or humanity, at all commensurate with the resources of the nation."

It is for the clarity and wisdom of such political and social generalizations as these that men turn back to Emerson, as they turn back to De Tocqueville and Bryce. The specific issues facing our American democracy seem to change overnight, but the fundamental problems remain. Emerson's faith in the democratic experiment seems to me as strong as that of Jefferson or Lincoln, but unlike those men, he has never moved the great masses of his countrymen. He is an individualist, and he still stimulates individuals rather than crowds. The Collectivists, for a hundred years now, have distrusted him, finding him lacking in what they call "the social sense." Even Woodberry called him "anti-social." He re-

fused to join his friends in the Brook Farm
community. He disliked to "join" anything, in fact;
preferring, like Thoreau, to "sign off" instead. All
the "Lo here!" and "Lo, there!" people seemed to
him volatile and transitory. I think he must have
liked Carlyle's grim saying: "The world's being
saved will not save us; nor the world's being lost
destroy us. We should look to ourselves."[6] If Emerson were alive in our day of "uplift" organizations
and "nation-wide hook-ups" he would be amazed that
anyone should count the number of radios and tele-
phones and motor-cars as real tests of civilization.
He would of course be intelligent enough to see
that hundreds of excellent organizations like the
Red Cross could not exist without the familiar pro-
cess of forming a committee and appointing a secretary and treasurer and passing resolutions and then
passing the hat,—but his heart would not be in it.
He was primarily interested in "the private person,"
and in democracy because he believed that that social
system, rather than any other, released the energies
of the private person. "Produce great persons," cried
his disciple Walt Whitman, "and the rest follows."
We do not really know whether the rest follows, for
we have not yet produced enough great persons to
test the theory. I think Emerson would enjoy a
letter I once read from a schoolboy describing his
first game of football in a new school: "Our opponents found a big hole in our line, and that hole was
me." That is one trouble with our American democracy: there is always a big hole somewhere in the

line! And Emerson, the most hopeful and inde-
fatigable of coaches,—though he may be a bit weak
in the general strategy and tactics of team-play,—is
forever heartening the courage of the individual
player. He is too shrewd not to know that to
strengthen the units is the only way thus far discovered of strengthening the line.

IV

I do not believe that Emerson was ever under any
illusion as to the nature of his influence and the character of his readers. We have already seen how he
told Carlyle that he fancied his readers were of "a
very quiet, plain, even obscure class." There is a still
more striking passage in his *Journals* (September 20,
1839) where he described the real audience for new
ideas:

"They are not organized into any conspiracy: they
do not vote, or print or meet together. They do not
know each other's faces or names. They are united
only in a common love of truth and love of its work.
They are of all conditions and natures. They are,
some of them, mean in attire, and some mean in
station, and some mean in body, having inherited
from their parents faces and forms scrawled with the
traits of every vice. Not in churches, or in courts, or
in large assemblies; not in solemn holidays, where
men were met in festive dress, have these pledged
themselves to new life, but in lonely and obscure
places, in servitude, in solitude, in solitary compunc-
tions and shames and fears, in disappointments, in

diseases, trudging beside the team in the dusty road, or drudging, a hireling in other men's cornfields, school-masters who teach a few children rudiments for a pittance, ministers of small parishes of the obscurer sects, lone women in dependent condition, matrons and young maidens, rich and poor, beautiful and hard-favoured, without conceit or proclamation of any kind, have silently given in their several adherence to a new hope."

The persons described in that passage may seem as queer as if they had come out of Robert Frost's poems. But the most curious parallel, even in its prose rhythm, is found in Rousseau's prefaces to his *Nouvelle Héloïse*, addressed to the *âme sensible*, to the solitary reader. There is the enduring audience, after all; as Rousseau and Wordsworth and Emerson had the genius to perceive. The superficial changes in the American reading public seem, indeed, to be startling, especially in that section of the country where Emerson first won his reputation. The majority of the population of his native State has long been made up of the foreign-born and their children. You may walk for hours through the streets of those industrial cities of Massachusetts where Emerson used to lecture, without seeing a single Yankee face. In spite of better schools and libraries, the average level of intelligence has temporarily declined. Fewer books are sold and read, in proportion to the population, than in Emerson's day. After Senator Lodge had delivered his Plymouth oration in 1920 I asked Mr. Arthur Lord of the Massachusetts Historical

Society,—a native of Plymouth,—whether Daniel Webster, who delivered the oration in 1820, did not have a more intelligent audience than Senator Lodge. "I know he did," said Mr. Lord. "I sent out the invitations to the 1920 celebration myself!"

And nevertheless, in spite of this temporary submergence of the old standards of thought and feeling in the industrial centers in New England, I will risk the assertion that if you go back a few miles from the railroads, and from the through motor routes with their filling stations and hot-dog shacks and blatant advertising signs, you will make a singular discovery. You will find, one at a time, thousands of solitary readers who know their Wordsworth and their Emerson quite as well as you do, and who get a quiet happiness from it. We do not look in the right places for the reading public. The foreign-born, as soon as they have a fair chance, can tell a good book from a poor one quite as quickly as the Mayflower Descendants. The other day the Finnish cook of a friend of mine asked her mistress, with whom I happened to be dining, if she might shake hands with me. I went out to the kitchen, with the puzzled mistress of the house, and discovered that the cook, who knew scarcely a word of English, had been reading *The Heart of Emerson's Journals* as translated and printed week by week in a Finnish newspaper in Fitchburg, Massachusetts. Professor Garrod of Oxford University told us last year in his "Harvard Lectures on Poetry" that Emerson is less widely read in England than he was thirty years ago, and

that "in Oxford if I am caught reading him, it is as
though I were caught reading the Bible." But it does
not appear that Emerson was ever much read at
Oxford, except by a few men in the undergraduate
days of Arnold and Clough. The men who read
Emerson and heard him gladly were the working
men, members of Mechanics Institutes in the West
and North of England and Scotland, the non-con-
formists, the radicals, the young women puzzled
about their careers, like Mary Ann Evans, who talked
Rousseau with Emerson the first time they met and
said afterward "He is the first man I have seen." It
was only here and there that he influenced young men
like Huxley and Tyndall. It was Tyndall who picked
up at a bookstall a copy of Emerson's *Nature* and
said long afterward to Moncure Conway: "I have
never ceased to read it; and if any one can be said
to have given the impulse to my mind, it is Emerson: whatever I have done the world owes to him."[7]

Professor Herman Grimm, one of the earliest
German admirers of Emerson, was extravagant, no
doubt, when he said that Emerson was like Shakespeare in that both could be read without any preparation. There must certainly be preparation, whether
it be in the mind of a Finnish cook or in the mind of
a Tyndall; but it is clearly impossible to draw any
social or racial lines of limitation around the influence of a literary artist. Once give him the safe-
guard of print, and he has his chance; and perhaps we
make too much of those obvious and temporary
changes in the public taste which make a writer go

out of fashion in one circle or country, and as inevitably, in due time, bring him into fashion in another.

In our own country, with its habit of swift forgetfulness of great public characters, we are often tempted to think that a writer's death marks the term of his influence. And indeed, it often does. When Emerson gave up lecturing, at last, through the weakness of old age, one source of his immediate power disappeared, as with the actor or the orator. That magical presence could fascinate men no more. But Americans of the twentieth century, who respect Emerson even when they do not read him, may perhaps be reminded that his death freed him from one handicap which he had carried throughout his public career. It is difficult for us to remember that for decades the very name "Emerson" was a newspaper joke, a synonym for absurdity and obscurity of thought. Mr. Howells, writing thirty years ago of his own early life as a journalist,[8] tells us: "It would be hard to persuade people now that Emerson once represented to the popular mind all that was hopelessly impossible, and that in a certain sort he was a national joke, the type of the incomprehensible, the byword of the poor paragrapher." Mr. Howells thought that it was really "Emerson's great fortune to have been mostly misunderstood, and to have reached the dense intelligence of his fellow men after a whole lifetime of perfectly simple and lucid appeal." It is fair to add that Emerson himself seems to have been quite as philosophical as Mr. Howells over his predicament, but that the handicap was serious no one can doubt. And now in a moment it was all over. Mr. Emerson was dead. The paragraphers turned elsewhere for amusement. Whether Emerson was as "simple and lucid" as he appeared to Mr. Howells, or as obscure and eccentric as he seemed to others, was henceforth to be settled, as every writer would wish to have it settled, by an appeal to the printed page.

V

Now it has become clear today that many of those printed pages,—in fact far more of them than was once realized,—are purely literary, written by a gifted literary artist rather than by a moralist, and that they may be read with the detached, timeless pleasure with which we read Lamb and Hazlitt. Emerson's sketch of Thoreau is as vivid and as enduring as Hazlitt's sketch of Coleridge. His portrait of old Dr. Ripley is as artistic as Lamb's picture of the "Old Benchers of the Middle Temple." Dozens of his lighter essays, delicate in touch and full of whimsical charm, were neglected by the nineteenth century in favor of the big motor-minded essays which admonish the reader to gird up his loins and "do something about it." These famous essays will always have their admirers, and justly so. Matthew Arnold's polemic essays won him a notoriety which he had failed to win as a poet and purely literary critic, and yet today his once-famous catchwords about British social ethics are worn threadbare by repetition, while his pages on Heine and Joubert, Obermann and Keats and Wordsworth are as ador-. ably fresh as ever. Professor Garrod, a most fastidious critic, thinks that no one, unless it be William James, has said plainly the "bare truth, that Emerson's greatness is preeminently that of a verbal artist. . . . The artist in him, the artist in words, was dominant—exiled from his verse to be the tyrant of his prose. Such a word-watcher, such a word-catcher, such a weigher-in-the-balance of niceties of rhythm and order, as well as of phrase, has seldom been."[9] Perhaps other twentieth century critics will make the same discovery. We are familiar with the distinction between "pure" and "applied" science. I suspect that many of Emerson's pages have been "applied" too much, and enjoyed too little.

Nevertheless it seems certain that his phrases, as well as his cardinal doctrine of individualism, will continue to be used as a corrective of certain tendencies of twentieth century society. He taught us long ago that "culture corrects the theory of success." That there are serious flaws in our current American theories of success no one can doubt. For a score of years past, group after group of young men, dissatisfied and embittered with "standardization" and "mass production" and other economic, social and educational tendencies, have been attacking them with weapons drawn from Emerson's arsenal of texts. Some of this caustic criticism has been sanative,—like Arnold's in England two generations ago,—and some of it has been merely reckless and clever, using Emerson's sharp-edged phrases without sharing either his fundamental faith in his country or his practical wisdom in selecting objects and methods of attack. "Can you convince the shoe interest," Emerson once asked, "or the iron interest, or the cotton interest, by reading passages from Milton or Montesquieu?" He himself never wasted his ammunition.

VI

Whether the coming generation will turn to Emerson's writings primarily for their beauty or primarily for their truth, no one can say, and guesses would be futile. Perhaps it makes little difference, for he seems certain, in any case, to be read. It is clear that the present swing in the current of scientific and philosophic thought is bringing Emerson's views afresh to the attention of the public. The drift away from positivism, from those mechanistic and deterministic theories so popular in the nineteenth century, is generally admitted. Here is a distinguished physicist, Sir Arthur Eddington, actually broadcasting a radio address in which he asserts that "materialism and determinism, those household gods of nineteenth century science, which believed that this world could be explained in mechanical and biological concepts as a well run machine, every cog of which moved in relation to other cogs, must be discarded by modern science, this to make room for a spiritual conception of the universe and man's place in it." Here is another English physicist, Sir James Jeans, declaring,

in a book which is at the moment a "best seller":[10]
"Today there is a wide measure of agreement, which
on the physical side of science approaches almost to
unanimity, that the stream of knowledge is heading
toward non-mechanical reality. The universe begins
to look more like a great thought than like a great
machine. Mind no longer appears as an accidental
intruder into the realm of matter; we are beginning
to suspect that we ought rather to hail it as the creator and governor of the realm of matter, not of
course our individual minds, but the mind in which
the atoms out of which our individual minds have
grown, exist as thoughts." A Yale professor points
out to us that all this is really "Platonism thrusting
itself above the surface of thought again."[11] In any
case it is a conception of the universe and of the relation of the individual mind to the universal
mind,—or, if one prefers the words, "the relation of
one's soul to the divine soul"—strikingly similar to
what Emerson has been saying all the time.

I do not mean, of course, that Emerson knew anything about twentieth century physics and chemistry
and astronomy. Probably he would be puzzled by
the vocabulary of our contemporary psychologists,
and certainly he would be too ignorant of mathemati-
cal logic to follow some of the subtle arguments of
Bergson and Whitehead, to say nothing of Einstein.
But in the general atmosphere of thought in which
such men are moving, Emerson would be perfectly
at home, in spite of his ignorance of the various

special languages there spoken. In creating this atmosphere of thought, these contemporary intellectual leaders are again making possible the mood in
which Emerson wrote,—a mood of spiritual awareness, of spiritual vigor. We have seen nothing like it
in the last fifty years. When Professor Norton, at the
Concord commemoration in 1903, tried to summarize Emerson's spiritual teaching in two sentences,
more than one listener to that delicate wearied voice
must have suspected that Norton was assessing values
in which he no longer believed; as if he were expounding, as had once been his professional duty,
the cosmology of Dante. This is what he said:[12]

"The essence of his [Emerson's] spiritual teaching seems to me to be comprised in three fundamental
articles,—first, that of the Unity of Being in God and
Man; second, that of the creation of the visible,
material world by Mind, and of its being the symbol
of the spiritual world; and third, that of the identity
and universality of moral law in the spiritual and
material universe. These truths are for him the basis
of life, the substance of religion, and the meaning of
the universe." In 1903 these words might easily have
been taken for an echo of yesterday's faith which no
one really believes will come back tomorrow. But tomorrow has dawned, and Norton's summary of
Emerson's faith seems far more typical of the current thought of the day than it did at the beginning
of the century.

VII

Many years ago, I happened to be lecturing on Emerson to a convocation of clergymen. Possibly, toward the end of the hour, I grew too extravagant in his praise. At any rate the chairman, who was the president of the local Theological Seminary, and who was seated with two or three other ministers on the long black haircloth sofa back of the pulpit, whispered to one of these gentlemen: "Brother Blank, as soon as the speaker finishes, please lead us in prayer. I had intended to ask you this evening, but there is a larger audience present this afternoon. And please introduce into your prayer this statement: 'Emerson, after all, had his limitations.'"

The lecturer, fortunately, was quite unaware of these whispered instructions. They may not have been quite sportsmanlike, but they suggest a truism that must not be overlooked. Emerson was singularly free from many of the grosser personal faults of literary men, but if he had had no limitations his character would lack outline and reality. As one studies the lists of these limitations, as they are set down by Emerson's biographers and in the memories of those who knew him well, they fall into two or three familiar categories.

The first, in fact, is too familiar: it stresses Emerson's limitations by comparing him with other men with whom there is no reason for a comparison. That is to say, you assert that Emerson is not somebody else. He had a knack for philosophizing, perhaps, but he was not a Descartes; a taste for science, but he was not a Pasteur; a zest for life, and yet no Rabelais; and so forth. One would have thought that Laurence Sterne had satirized this type of criticism once for all in *Tristram Shandy*, where the connoisseur declares of "the grand picture" that there is "not one principle of the pyramid in any one group!—nothing of the coloring of Titian,—the expression of Rubens,—the grace of Raphael,—the purity of Domenichino,—the corregiescity of Corregio,"—and so forth.

A second limitation, and this is a real one for some readers, is that Emerson often gives an impression of aloofness. If he had never written those early and unsatisfactory essays on "Love" and "Friendship," if he had not bewailed so often his lack of animal spirits, and if all his unpublished letters were accessible to the public, there would be much less said about his coldness. But it is true that he loved solitude, and that even when he invites you to take a walk with him, he likes the high, bare places above the timber-line. Many of his devoted admirers, like Henry James the elder, felt that they could not really get at him. He was "a literal divine presence in the house with me" James testified, but "any average old dame in a horse-car would have satisfied my intellectual rapacity just as well as Emerson." That is to say, when the ebullient and delightful half-Irish Swedenborgian felt most like talking,—and that was always,—Emerson grew more and more silent. Alcott had the same experience, and Margaret Fuller,—bound-

less talkers both. As they expanded, Emerson con-
tracted, to the zero point. It was irritating. Yet this
was the very person who enjoyed meeting the plain
farmers and tavern-keepers in the Social Circle, was
curious to visit a rough miners' theater in San Francisco, liked to read French novels when riding on the
Pennsylvania railroad, and joyfully attended in Den-
ver a melodrama entitled "Marriage by Moonlight;
or, the Wild-Cat's Revenge."[13] Why did he make intellectual interlocutors so conscious of his isolation of
spirit, his fastidious, aristocratic withdrawnness into
himself? Why could he not assume, even if he did
not feel, a Rotarian warmth?

A third limitation, noted by many critics, and
especially by George Woodberry, is that in stressing
his doctrine of individualism Emerson underesti-
mates or even eliminates social institutions. He becomes "blind to the life of humanity in the race."
Obsessed by the significance of the present moment,
how could he feel the vast sweep of the current of
history? He read history for useful and picturesque
anecdotes of the single person, but aside from this,
"all was picture as he passed." Of the actual forces
conditioning the activities of men in successive epoch,
how little he seemed aware! He read Burke, but he
never really felt him, except as a rhetorician. How
much Hegel might have taught him, or even his
utterly non-Hegelian friend Carlyle! I should not
dream of calling Emerson, as Woodberry does, "anti-
Christian, anti-scientific, anti-social," but I think
there is more force in the last adjective than in the

other two. In *English Traits*, one of his most brilliant journalistic performances, he showed a keen
appreciation of many British institutions like the
Established Church and the Law Courts and the
Parliament. From 1850 on, his perception of the
vital forces underlying American institutions grew
deeper, but in the earlier essays, there is undoubtedly
a reckless and anarchic individualism which still re-
pels many readers whose loyalty he might otherwise
win.

This individualistic mood of the 1830's and '40's
has recalled to many readers the similar mood of the
Renaissance. But neither Rabelais nor Emerson
would wish to be taken literally. Both of them say
"Do what thou wilt," but that motto in Rabelais
was written for a select company of noble ladies and
gentlemen who were seeking the good life, and the
high-minded Emerson wrote it for young men whom
he assumed to be as high-minded as himself. In each
of these historical eras it proved a dangerous doctrine for the moral weakling, an intoxicant for
second-rate minds.

It is in his relation to historical Christianity, of
course, that this unguarded individualism of Emerson's, this insensitiveness to the actual experience
of our Western civilization, continues chiefly to be
felt. His intellectual rebellion against much of the
orthodox Christian dogma was clear enough after
1832, but his personal tenderness toward the ancient
modes of thought and feeling has often been overlooked. In many a passage from his letters, *Journals*

and lesser known writings he betrays his sympathy for what he called "the old religion." In "The Sovereignty of Ethics," for example, we find these sentences: "The creeds into which we were initiated in childhood and youth no longer hold their old place in the minds of thoughtful men, but they are not nothing to us, and we hate to have them treated with contempt. There is so much that we do not know that we give to these suggestions the benefit of the doubt. . . . I confess our later generation appears ungirt, frivolous, compared with the religions of the last or Calvinistic age. . . . The religion of seventy years ago was an iron belt to the mind, giving it concentration and force." And in his address "The Preacher" we read: "The Catholic Church has been immensely rich in men and influences. Augustine, à Kempis, Fénelon, breathe the very spirit which now fires you. So with Cudworth, More, Bunyan. I agree with them more than I disagree. I agree with their heart and motives; my discontent is with their limitations and surface and language."

In the face of such passages,—and the list might be greatly extended,—I should not dare to call Emerson "anti-Christian." Abraham Lincoln's widow is reported to have used an odd phrase about her husband: "He was not a technical Christian." Probably she meant that Mr. Lincoln had never joined any church. Whether Emerson was "a technical Christian" is a matter that we must leave to the theologians, although he would have challenged sharply their right to decide. But it is obvious that this gentlest of iconoclasts was and still is terribly annoying to all literal-minded persons, all formalists and pigeon-holers. What can be more trying to such people than a spiritually-minded pronouncer of opinions who refuses to define,—not being interested in definitions,—and who deprecates argument because of his confessed inability to argue? In his well known letter to the Rev. Henry Ware, Jr., he admits: "I do not know what arguments mean in reference to any expression of a thought. I delight in telling what I think, but if you ask how I dare say so, or why it is so, I am the most helpless of mortal men."[14] This was no clever assumption of the rôle of Socratic humility and ignorance; it was what Emerson actually felt.

It seems to me that Emerson's real limitation here is not in his mode of apprehending truth,—for many kinds of buckets go down into that deep well,—but rather in his lack of dramatic imagination. He could not put himself in the place of the average church-goer. I confess that I still follow with keen enjoyment the red-hot theological pamphlets that were fired back and forth over the "Divinity School Address" by such redoubtable combatants as Andrews Norton and George Ripley and Theodore Parker and the Princeton professors, Dod and Alexander. But the most practically effective answer to Emerson's views, although he is not mentioned, may be illustrated by a sermon preached by Alexander Young at the ordination of George E. Ellis in 1840: "The

Christian minister is to preach the declarations and statements, the doctrines and principles of the Gospel. In his view, religion is identified with Christianity, and he values Christianity because it gives him assurance of certain truths which he regards as of infinite importance. These truths constitute his religion. . . . All our knowledge of Christ and Christianity is derived, not from consciousness or intuition, but from outward revelation. It is not innate, spontaneous, and original with us, but extrinsic, derived, superinduced. . . . Once admit that the New Testament does not contain all the principles of spiritual truth . . . and you open the door to all sorts of loose and crude speculations. . . . The old heathen sages, it is true, stumbled on some fortunate conjectures, and made some happy guesses, but they could assert nothing with assurance; they could not speak with *certainty* and *authority*."[15]

Dr. Young expresses here the average mind of the ordinary believer in the Gospel, century after century. Emerson failed to make allowance for it, partly because of his indifference to dogma and creed, his unconcern for historicity, his heedlessness of any form of authority, but partly, also, because it was hard for him to identify himself, even dramatically and for the moment, with the mental habits of the great mass of men.

Two other illustrations of this mental isolation or insulation must be mentioned briefly. One of them was his belief, which he shared with the Neo-Platonists, that God is supra-personal. Now we all

use the word "person" every day, but really to define it, as applied to the Deity, challenges the intellect of a Jonathan Edwards. Emerson felt that
the word "personal" implied limitations. Did not
the very word *persona* once mean an actor's mask,—
a disguise, an assumed or imputed character? Emerson knew the inveterate tendency of humanity to
create a Deity in its own image. Had not Spinoza
said: "I believe that a triangle, if it could speak,
would say that God is eminently triangular, and a
circle that the Divine Nature is eminently circular,
and thus would every one ascribe his own attributes
to God."[16] It was for this reason that Emerson
declared "The soul knows no persons"; a sentence
which gave great offense to many religious people.
He hedges brilliantly, it is true, in the essay on
"Self-Reliance": "In your metaphysics you have
denied personality to the Deity, yet when the devout
motions of the soul come, yield to them heart and
life, though they should clothe God with shape and
color." Yet this reminds one of what President
Patton once said about picking up something with
your emotions after you have thrown it out of the
window with your intellect.

To a group of theological students who found his
view of the impersonality of God "desolating and
ghastly" Emerson explained: "I deny personality
to God because it is too little, not too much. Life,
personal life, is faint and cold to the energy of
God."[17] Elliot Cabot, who had pursued philosophical studies, remarks that "Emerson's denial of

God's personality was only an affirmation of the infinitude of His nature, transcending all the efforts of human imagination and understanding to compass and express it."[18] We may leave the matter there, but it is only too evident that in such metaphysical speculations Emerson expected his hearers to go with him not only up above the timber-line, but beyond the sky-line. He forgot the uncounted millions of men, some of them far better trained in philosophy than he was, who cling to the first two words of the Lord's Prayer.

The other illustration of Emerson's mental habit of isolating himself from common human experience is found, as all his readers are aware, in the slight attention he pays to the problem of evil. In minimizing its significance in the general scheme of things, he again follows Plotinus rather than St. Augustine and Calvin. It is true that some of his early diaries are in contradiction to the tone of his later essays. At nineteen he writes (I, 246) "There *is* a huge and disproportionate abundance of *evil* on earth." When he decides to enter the ministry he speaks of that calling as "the service of God and the War against Sin" (I, 367). In the happiness over his engagement to Ellen Tucker, he asks: "Will God forgive me my sins?" (II, 261). But he outgrew this vocabulary and mood so completely that in his later life the puzzled Henry James the elder speaks of his "innocent" and "unfallen" friend as "utterly unconscious of himself as either good or evil. He had no conscience, in fact, and lived by perception, which is an altogether lower or less spiritual faculty."[19]

However that may be, the whole burden of Emerson's mature thought places little stress upon evil. "The intellect names it shade, absence of light, and no essence. The conscience must feel it as essence, essential evil. This it is not; it has an objective existence, but no subjective."[20] That is to say,—if I understand him rightly,—while there is such a thing as evil, it is temporary, transient, and it is wiser not to think too much about it! As Martin Luther remarked cheerfully: "You cannot keep the crows from flying over your head, but you can keep them from building nests in your hair." We are very far, evidently, from the mood of Hawthorne or the mood of Carlyle, though both of these literary artists were emancipated from traditional Puritan theology. We are much nearer to Browning's "The evil is null, is naught, is silence implying sound,"—a doctrine which the excellent Abt Vogler might have found in Plato.

We are not here concerned, however, with literary parallels, but with the plain fact that Emerson's inability or unwillingness to grapple with the problem of evil has disconcerted many of his warmest admirers like John Morley, and made him seem more than ever insulated from contact with the actual world. The twentieth century, in and out of the churches, seems far less concerned than the nineteenth century with theories about sin, and it may prove that Emerson's way of looking up and not down, forward and not back, will be counted practically wise although philosophically inadequate. But to his own generation, certainly, it looked as if he had failed to come to close grip with actualities, had been tranquilly aloof from what the second Henry James calls somewhere our immitigable mortal predicament. There is a single paragraph in Newman's *Apologia*,—beginning "To consider the world in its length and breadth,"—which faces the tragic mysteries of human life more squarely than any page of Emerson.

VIII

We turn finally to those traits of Emerson's mind and character which now seem perdurable,—unaffected by transient modes of thought or by the currents of social and literary change. Only one observer had the opportunity of studying Emerson closely, week after week, in the solitude of the primeval forest. That was W. J. Stillman, the artist and journalist, who in his *Autobiography*,—now an almost forgotten book,—has recorded the impression made upon him, in those unique circumstances, by Emerson's personality. Writing long after all the members of the Adirondack Club were dead, and the forest itself burnt and pillaged, Stillman testifies that "Emerson looms up in that Arcadian dream more and more the dominant personality. It is as character and not as accomplishment or education, that he holds his own in all comparisons with his contemporaries, the fine, crystallized mind, the keen, clear-faceted thinker and seer. I loved more Agassiz and Lowell, but we shall have many a Lowell and Agassiz before we see Emerson's like again. Attainments will be greater, and discovery and accomplishments will surpass themselves as we go on, but to *be*, as Emerson was, is absolute and complete existence."[21]

These words, written thirty years ago, express a timeless truth. To *be*,—that is all; whether on the banks of the Ganges or the Ilyssus or the Concord River, makes little difference. Today we study Emerson through the printed page, and there we recognize, though perhaps not as clearly as our successors will, a literary artist, in some respects an incomparable master of words. Yet behind the words—as with Francis of Assisi and Gandhi of India—there is something which eludes words and makes the printed page a mere suggestion of a spirit, an attitude, a way of envisaging life. The mere weighing of literary qualities does not touch the essence of Emerson. There is an imponderable personal force in this man, an emanation of spiritual energy.

That this personal force is now recognized by an ever increasing number of individuals, representing differing civilizations in the Orient, upon the continent of Europe and in the United States, is beyond question. To find precise terms with which to describe the nature of this influence is not easy, but the words "poise" and "serenity" suggest it. No one will deny that these qualities were never more needed than today.

As to the intellectual side of contemporary life,
I quote President Angell of Yale. When the American Philosophical Society, not long ago, asked many
leaders of thought to summarize the world's intellectual needs, President Angell replied: "Perhaps
the most pressing intellectual need, in the western
world at least, is represented by the acquirement of
such poise as comes from a genuine coordination of
the great sub-divisions of thought. These sub-divisions have become so highly specialized, so sep-
aratistic and so self-conscious, not to say self-com-
placent, that the genuinely philosophical outlook of
life and its problems, an outlook which presupposes
inclusive vision and genuine insight, has become
utterly impossible." Not "utterly" impossible, one
is tempted to add, for a man who shares to some
degree the inclusive vision and the poise of an
Emerson.

On the artistic side of contemporary life I might
quote any of the innumerable American pessimists.
But they forget that our fashionable post-War cyn-
icism was exactly paralleled by the European post-
Revolutionary and post-Napoleonic pessimism of a
century ago, and is likely to prove as transient. But
I prefer to quote from the author of *The Cherry
Orchard*, because his diagnosis of artistic sterility
goes deeper. In Chekov's *Letters to His Family*
(p. 319) there is this passage:

"Science and technical knowledge are passing
through a great period now, but for our sort it is
a flabby, stale, and dull time. . . . The causes of

this are not to be found in our stupidity, our lack of talent, or our insolence. . . . We lack 'something,' that is true, and that means that, lift the robe of our muse, and you will find within an empty void. Let me remind you that the writers, who we say are for all time or are simply good, and who intoxicate us, have one common and very important characteristic; they are going towards something and are summoning you towards it, too, and you feel not with your mind, but with your whole being, that they have some object, just like the ghost of Hamlet's father, who did not come and disturb the imagination for nothing. Some have more immediate objects—the abolition of serfdom, the liberation of their country, politics, beauty, or simply vodka, like Denis Davydov; others have remote objects—God, life beyond the grave, the happiness of humanity, and so on. The best of them are realists and paint life as it is, but, through every line's being soaked in the consciousness of an object, you feel, besides life as it is, the life which ought to be, and that captivates you. And we? We! We paint life as it is, but beyond that—nothing at all . . . flog us and we can do no more! We have neither immediate nor remote aims, and in our soul there is a great empty space. We have no politics, we do not believe in revolution, we have no God, we are not afraid of ghosts, and I personally am not afraid even of death and blindness. One who wants nothing, hopes for nothing, and fears nothing, cannot be an artist. . . ."

Those words, so exact in their rendering of one

phase of contemporary literature, although they
were written in 1892, may explain why so many
readers are turning to Emerson as a man who is
going towards something and summoning you towards it, too. I am not offering Emerson's writings
as a tract for the times. Tracts for the times go
swiftly out of date. But I know that the mere mention
of Emerson's name, like the name of George Washington, reinforces in many men their belief in the
power of the will, their faith in the unseen.

Let us end, as we began, with a paradox out of
old Concord. Henry Thoreau, an unashamed individualist, was bent throughout his short life upon
a single quest;—pathetic and futile as it seemed to
most of his neighbors, but heroic as we see it today,
—since it was the quest of spiritual perfection. He
uttered, like Emerson, many a paradox; in fact he
believed, as Emerson did, in that most incredible and
yet best attested of all paradoxes: "Ask, and ye
shall receive; seek, and ye shall find." He wrote in
his diary at the age of twenty-three these words,—
not unfitting to remember as we take leave of Emerson: "I do not judge men by anything they can do.
Their greatest deed is the impression they make on
me. Some serene, inactive men can do everything."

NOTES

CHAPTER ONE

1. Cooke, **G. W.** *Ralph Waldo Emerson; His Life, Writings and Philosophy.* Boston, 1881.
2. Parish, Olive Slade. *The French View of Emerson.* Unpublished M.A. thesis, Yale University, 1929.
3. Cabot, James Elliot. *A Memoir of Ralph Waldo Emerson.* 2 vols. Boston, 1887.
4. Emerson, Edward W. *Emerson in Concord.* Boston, 1888.
5. Holmes, Oliver Wendell. *Ralph Waldo Emerson.* Boston, 1885.
6. James, William. *Letters.* 2 vols. Boston, 1920. Vol. II, p. 194.
7. Michaud, R. *Autobiographie d' Emerson, d'aprés son Journal intime.* Colin, Paris, 1914-1918.
8. Perry, Bliss. *The Heart of Emerson's Journals.* Boston, 1926.
9. Russell, Philips. *Emerson: The Wisest American.* New York, 1929.
10. Gay, R. M. *Emerson; A Study of the Poet as Seer.* New York, 1928.
11. Michaud, R. *La Vie inspirée d'Emerson.* Paris, 1930. The title of the English translation is *Emerson; the Enraptured Yankee.* New York, 1930.
12. Brooks, Van Wyck. *Emerson and Others.* New York. 1927.
13. Hotson, C. P. *Emerson and Swedenborg.* Harvard Ph.D. thesis, 1929. Portions of this thesis, under the title *Emerson and the Doctrine of Correspondence,* were printed in four numbers of the *New Church Review,* Boston, January-October.
14. Carpenter, F. I. *Emerson and Asia.* Cambridge, Harvard University Press, 1930.
15. Gordon, George A. "Emerson as a Religious Influence." *Atlantic Monthly,* May 1903.
16. Goddard, H. C. *Studies in New England Transcendentalism.* New York, Columbia University Press, 1908. See also Professor Goddard's chapter on Transcendentalism in the *Cambridge History of American Literature,* Vol. I.
17. Essay on "Worship."
18. White, K. C. R. *The American Lyceum.* Harvard Ph.D. dissertation, 1918, unpublished.

19. *Records of a Life-long Friendship*, Boston and New York, 1910. p. 5.

20. Lowell, J. R. "Emerson the Lecturer," *My Study Windows*. Boston, 1886. See also the article "Mr. Emerson in the Lecture Room," by Annie Fields, *Atlantic*, June 1883.

CHAPTER TWO

1. *Some Reminiscences of the Life of Samuel Kirkland Lothrop*. Edited by T. K. Lothrop. Cambridge, 1888.

2. Michaud, R. "A French Friend and Inspirer of Emerson." *University of California Chronicle*, April 1921. See also the chapter on Murat in Michaud's *Autour d'Emerson*, Paris, 1924.

3. *Journals*, II, 259.

4. In *Miscellanies*.

5. Reprinted in Cabot, II, 685.

6. Cabot, II, 633.

7. Now in possession of his granddaughter, Mrs. Archibald Henderson, Chapel Hill, N. C.

8. Conway, Moncure D. *Emerson at Home and Abroad*. Boston, 1882. p. 335.

9. Stillman, W. J. *Autobiography of a Journalist*. 2 vols. Boston, 1901. Vol. I, p. 254. See also Stillman's article "the Philosopher's Camp," *Century*, August 1893.

16. *Letters from Emerson to a Friend*. Boston, 1899.

CHAPTER THREE

1. Jones, Rufus M. *Studies in Mystical Religion*. London and New York, 1909.

2. Underhill, Evelyn. *Mysticism*. New York, 1911. *The Life of the Spirit and the Life of Today*. London, 1922.

3. Inge, W. R. *Christian Mysticism*. London, 1899
    Personal Idealism and Mysticism. London, 1907.
    The Philosophy of Plotinus. 2 vols. London, 1923.

4. *Journals*, I, 361.

5. *Journals*, II, 170.

6. See Fox's *Journal* for 1648. Emerson quoted a portion of this passage in his unpublished lecture on "George Fox," 1835.

7. Underhill, E. *Mysticism*, p. 121.

8. Norton, C. E. *Letters*. 2 vols. Boston and New York, 1913. Vol. I, p. 513.

9. See Emerson's memoir of her in *Lectures and Biographical Sketches*, and the essay on *Mary Moody Emerson* by the late

George Tolman of Concord, privately printed by Edward W. Forbes, Cambridge, 1929.

10. Carpenter, Chapters III and IV. Also, Harrison, J. S., *The Teachers of Emerson*. New York, 1910.
11. Carpenter, p. 43.
12. Inge, W. R. *Plotinus*, Vol. II, pp. 160-162.
13. Cabot, II, 471.
14. Hotson, C. P. "Sampson Reed, a Teacher of Emerson," *N.E. Quarterly*, Vol. II, No. 2, 1929.
15. See Chapter I, n. 13.
16. *Journals*, VIII, 33.
17. Frothingham, O. B. *Transcendentalism in New England*. New York, 1876.
18. Cooke, G. W. *Poets of Transcendentalism*. Boston and New York, 1903.
19. See Goddard, *supra*.
20. Riley, Woodbridge. *American Thought*. New York, 1915.
21. Cabot, I, 218.
22. *Journals*, III, 236.
23. A complete list of these books is printed in the Appendix to Clara E. Sears's *Bronson Alcott's Fruitlands*, Boston, 1915.
24. A list is given in Carpenter, p. 263.
25. Compare Woodberry, G. E., *Emerson*, p. 164.
26. Carpenter, pp. 124-127.
27. Harrison, *Teachers of Emerson*, p. 275.
28. See Edward Emerson's note in *Letters and Social Aims*, p. 412.
29. See the note in the privately printed *Essays, Addresses and Poems* of Edward W. Emerson. Riverside Press, Cambridge, 1930, p. 283.
30. Bonar, James. *Moral Sense*. London, 1930.
31. Cabot, I, 236.
32. Told me by the late Francis J. Garrison, who was present at the meeting.
33. From "Merlin."

CHAPTER FOUR

1. Norton, *Letters*, II. 12. There is a much fuller discussion of Emerson's "inexperience" in the passage from Norton's journal describing his talks with Emerson on shipboard. See Vol. I of the *Letters*, pp. 502-514.
2. Wendell, Barrett. *Literary History of America*, p. 327.
3. *Education of Henry Adams*. Boston, 1918, p. 35.

4. From the Concord "Address on the Fugitive Slave Law," May 3, 1851; in *Miscellanies*.

5. *Journals*, VIII, 236.

6. "The Hero as Man of Letters."

7. Conway, p. 150.

8. Howells, W. D. *Literary Friends and Acquaintance*. New York, 1902, p. 61.

9. Garrod, H. W. "Emerson," in *New England Quarterly*, Vol. III, No. 1, 1930.

10. Jeans, Sir James. *The Mysterious Universe*. London and New York, 1930, p. 158.

11. Northrop, F. C. S. "Physics and Platonism," in *Saturday Review*, New York, December 27, 1930.

12. *Emerson Centenary in Concord*. Riverside Press, 1903. p. 49.

13. Thayer, James Bradley. *A Western Journey with Mr. Emerson*. Boston, 1884, p. 28.

14. Perry, Bliss. *Selections from Emerson's Prose Works*. Boston and New York, 1926. p. 277.

15. Frothingham, O. B. *Boston Unitarianism*. New York, 1890. p. 169.

16. *Letters* of Spinoza, quoted in Durant's *Story of Philosophy*. New York, 1926. p. 192.

17. *Journals*, March 4, 1838.

18. Cabot, I, 343.

19. *Literary Remains of Henry James*, edited by William James. Boston, 1885. p. 299.

20. Essay on "Experience."

21. *Autobiography*, p. 256.

CHRONOLOGICAL TABLE

1803. Emerson born, in Boston, May 25.

1813-17. At the Boston Latin School.

1817-21. At Harvard College.

1821-28. Teaching school and studying Divinity at Harvard.

1829. Pastor of Second Church of Boston. Married, September, to Ellen Louisa Tucker.

1831. Death of his wife (February).

1832. Resigned his pastorate (September). Sailed for Europe (December).

1833. Returned from Europe (October).

1834. Death of Edward Emerson in Porto Rico.

1835. Married to Lydia Jackson (September).

1836. Charles Emerson died (May). *Nature* published (September). Emerson's son Waldo born (October).

1837. *Phi Beta Kappa Address* (*The American Scholar;* August 31).

1838. *Divinity School Address* (July 15).

1841. *Essays, First Series.*

1842. His son Waldo died (January). Editor of *Dial* (1842-44).

1844. *Essays, Second Series.*

1847. *Poems.* Second visit to Europe.

1850. *Representative Men.*

1856. *English Traits.*

1860. *Conduct of Life.*

1867. *May Day* (poems).

1870. *Society and Solitude.*

1872. House burned; third visit to Europe.

1875. *Letters and Social Aims.*

1882. Died at Concord, April 27.